To Tom and Beth
[signature]
I Sam. 12:24

Yanga, the Miracle Village

Yanga, the Miracle Village

a sequel to "Battle for Yanga"

V. Ben Kendrick

Foreword by David Moore

REGULAR BAPTIST PRESS
1300 North Meacham Road
P.O. Box 95500
Schaumburg, Illinois 60195

Library of Congress Cataloging in Publication Data
Kendrick, V   Ben
    Yanga, the Miracle Village
    "A sequel to Battle for Yanga."
    1. Missionary stories   2. Banda (African people)—
Fiction. I. Title.
PS3561.E4233Y3 1983   813'.54   83-11033
ISBN 0-87227-095-5

Yanga, the Miracle Village
© 1983
Regular Baptist Press
Schaumburg, Illinois
Printed in U.S.A.
All rights reserved

Dedication

It is a privilege to dedicate this book to Dr. Allan E. Lewis, the beloved president of Baptist Mid-Missions. Born in a mud hut in the jungles of Angola, Africa, to missionary parents, Allan Lewis grew up in the exciting atmosphere of missions. His lengthy service in two pastorates and as mission president has made him a source of help and strength to thousands around the world. Only eternity will show the final results of the faithful ministry of this choice servant.

"The good news of the Gospel is only good news if it reaches the lost in time" (Allan E. Lewis).

V. Ben Kendrick

Acknowledgment

To Sallie McElwain, for her excellent work in typing, proofreading and other helps in preparing the book manuscript.

Contents

Foreword		9
Introduction		11
1	Harassment	13
2	Hot Dogs for Dinner	17
3	Strange Turn of Events	23
4	Come Back, Mr. Duval	27
5	Paul Returns	31
6	Wedding News	35
7	Caterpillar Sauce	40
8	Disturbing News	45
9	Snake!	49
10	Not My Will	53
11	Superstition	57
12	On Target—Djabalo	61
13	The Amazing Chief Paul	66
14	Miracle at 'Good News'	71
15	Join the Club	77
16	'Hello, Mr. Duval'	82
17	A Burden Kindled	86
18	A Double Wedding	91
19	Another Preaching Post	95
20	Congratulations, Paul	100
21	Car Trouble	104
22	Malaria	109
23	Tragedy at Good News	114
24	Emergency Ward	119
25	Marie's Decision	124

26	Two Letters	129
27	Tene's Spear Returns	134
28	Calling Dr. Simms	140
29	Questions and Answers	145
30	Unwelcomed Visitor	151
31	Chief Paul's Gift	157
32	The Last Sheep	163

Foreword

Half a lifetime is not long enough to know V. Ben Kendrick, missionary, author and personal friend. In this, his latest gift to the Christian reader, we have a worthy sequel to *Battle for Yanga*.

The writer's ministry gives evidences of the continued blessing of God throughout a missionary career of twenty-one years in the Central African Republic; and, in more recent years, coordinator of deputation in the home office of Baptist Mid-Missions. As mission executive and sought-after speaker, Ben is well-known to both pastors and missionaries, as well as churches and Christian colleges across our country. So many of us have been touched by his vitality and warmth as we have shared together in the work of the ministry. The years have provided a growing appreciation for Ben as a writer of never-to-be-forgotten missionary stories. *Yanga, the Miracle Village*, is another example of this kind of writing at its best, as expressed by one who is daily caught up in the Biblical compulsion of missions.

In more recent years I have known Ben in that even more personal relationship of a local church family. He has served faithfully in several leadership capacities in his home church.

We look forward to still other forthcoming titles to be added to a growing list of God-honoring books about missions by this gifted author.

Dr. David Moore, Pastor
Cedar Hill Baptist Church
Cleveland, Ohio

Introduction

Most Bible-believing Christians have a concept of missions as proclaimed in the divine commission. This book will enlarge that concept by giving practical application and emotion to missions. In the Sermon on the Mount, our Lord showed how the Commandments were misapplied because the spirit of the Commandment was not understood. The real heartbeat of missions is discovered in the spirit of the divine commission. This book opens our understanding of the missionary's ministry on the field. It reveals the real spirit of missions.

No one is better qualified to give this insight into missions than Dr. V. Ben Kendrick. Many years as a missionary laid the foundation. Additional experience as a leader in missions has prepared him to reach hearts with the need and ministry of reaching others.

The message of this book will not only thrill the reader, but it can be used to enhance his ministry. Sunday School teachers, Vacation Bible School teachers and youth workers will find it valuable in teaching missions to their students. A deeper insight into the ministry of missions will add a new dimension to anyone's ministry.

James F. Dersham
Managing Editor
Regular Baptist Press

1
Harassment

The look on Martin's face told Marie Blanc that something was wrong. For several weeks she had noticed a change in her husband's behavior but had been reluctant to say anything to him. Martin fumbled nervously with the letter he held. Now and then he would glance at it, slowly shaking his head, obviously in deep thought.

"What . . . what is it, Martin?" asked Marie. "Is something wrong?" Concerned, she walked across the room to where her husband sat and gently placed her hand on his shoulder. Martin stared at the letter, and Marie sensed he was searching for words to answer her. Slowly he raised his head, fear evident in his eyes. He held the letter out in front of him.

"It's the Party, honey. They've been after me for three weeks to rejoin them. Now they say that if we don't return within the next two weeks, they will do us harm. We both know what that means."

Marie Blanc knew the letter was not a bluff—she had grown up exposed to communism. Her French parents had been active members of the Communist Party ever since she could remember. It had not been unusual for visiting Party leaders to stay overnight in her parent's home. Marie was seventeen years old when she first joined the Party. Because of her dedication and promotion of the cause of communism, she was among two hundred other young French men and women chosen to take special training in Russia. While in Moscow she had made the acquaintance of Martin Blanc, a handsome young man from Central Africa.

"They mean what they say, Martin," said the anxious wife as she sat down beside her husband. She reached over and took him by the hand. "But the Lord will take care of us. He has done so many wonderful things for us since we have known Him. I'm sure we will see Him work something out for us."

"I know He will, Marie. I guess I'm just human enough to want our happiness to continue without any disruptions. But because we're not in Heaven yet, there will be difficulties that arise in our lives."

"These past weeks since we've come to know Christ have been wonderful," Marie sighed. "I will long remember how you came home from Africa with the news that you had accepted Christ as your Savior. I couldn't believe what I was hearing or seeing."

"I know," said Martin. "To think I went to convert my people to communism, and in turn was converted to Christ through the testimonies of our missionary friends and my own people."

The young husband squeezed his wife's hand and smiled. "And then God worked in your heart and saved you. Praise the Lord for what He has done for us."

"That's why I say we don't have to fear the Party, Martin. Our God is able to protect us. If it's His will that we die, then we will die. Don't be afraid, Martin. We're in this together. We'll trust the Lord for His perfect will to be done."

Marie's words brought relief to Martin. It had been all he could do the past three weeks to keep from telling her of the harassment he had endured from the Communists.

Since his father had been a French-government man, Martin had many advantages over the other African children. Most French-government men who took African women for wives wanted their children to have every opportunity that full-blooded French children had. As soon as Martin was old enough, he was sent to the capital city to attend French school. After finishing his secondary training, his father sent him to Paris to attend college, where he was first exposed to the Communist Party. Some of the students in his dorm invited him to attend a rally on campus. Liking what he heard, Martin decided to learn more about the doctrines of Marxism. It wasn't long before he was attending the monthly meetings.

Martin was taken by surprise one morning when a French Communist Party leader approached him as he came out of his dorm.

"Hello, Martin," spoke the young Frenchman briskly. "I've come to make you a proposal."

Martin recognized his visitor, having seen him in some of the Party's meetings. Surprised, he asked, "What is your proposal?" Martin had been exposed to the Party long enough to know that idle conversation was not appreciated.

"We want you to go to Moscow. We have been observing you and believe you can be of much use to the Party. We will train you and pay you for your services."

"When do you want me to go?"

"Next week. Special sessions begin two weeks from now. We have everything arranged for you. We will see that you receive your diploma from this university even though you don't finish your studies here."

Martin Blanc arrived in Moscow the following week. He was accompanied by a young Russian who was introduced to him at the airport just minutes before the plane's departure from Paris. Unknown to Martin, seating had been arranged so that the Russian would sit beside him. Conversation was impossible since the stranger didn't speak any French or at least pretended not to know any. At the airport in Moscow, two men hustled Martin off in a car to a walled complex of buildings.

Martin's first two months in Russia were spent mostly in private counseling sessions with experienced professors of communism. Little did he realize at the time that he was under twenty-four-hour surveillance. Any opposition to communism during those crucial eight weeks could have meant imprisonment or even death.

After his successful review with the counselors, Martin was allowed to attend class with others who had likewise been screened. Marie Boneau was one of those chosen for this indoctrination. She had grown up in the Party in Paris, but surprisingly had never met Martin in the French capital. The second week after they met, they received permission to date each other. In ten months, they were married. It was no surprise to them, after their training was over, to receive an assignment for Central Africa. What better way was there to infiltrate the large Banda tribe than to send one of their own people among them? Martin Blanc was perfect for the role.

A week before they were to leave for Africa, Marie decided she would stay in Paris until her husband established himself within the tribe. The presence of a white woman with Martin could possibly work against them. It was best not to take any chances for the sake of the Party.

The smell of fresh coffee and the rattle of china brought Martin out of his thoughts. "What should we do, Marie? Should we share this with our missionary friends? I know they would want to pray for us."

"I really don't know," answered Marie. "Maybe we should keep it to ourselves for now. If things get any worse, we can tell them."

That night Martin lay awake long into the night thinking about the day's events. "Father," he prayed silently, "thank You for Marie. She has been such a good help to me today. I ask You, dear Father, to watch over us. Protect us from the Communists." Martin's eyes became moist with tears. "And, Lord, open the way for Marie and me to go to Bible school this fall. My people need to hear Your Word. Please give us the privilege of teaching it among them someday."

The light shining through the curtains touched Martin's face. He opened his eyes to see that Marie had already awakened and was busy getting breakfast. The sound of sizzling bacon prompted him to get up and join her.

"Good morning," came Marie's cheerful voice when she heard the approaching footsteps. "I've never seen you sleep so soundly."

"It must be from the relief of sharing with you the Party's recent contacts with me," responded Martin. "I don't know how I can tell them any stronger than I already have that we don't want anything to do with them. I guess all we can do is wait and see what happens."

As the couple bowed their heads to thank the Lord for their food, there was a knock on the door. Martin looked across the table at Marie. He was certain her thoughts agreed with his—was this someone from the Party?

2
Hot Dogs

The small village of Yanga One, deep in the heart of Africa, had been buzzing with excitement for almost a year. Chief Paul, who had been converted ten months earlier at the mission station twenty miles away, had directed the believers in his village, with the help of missionaries Ken and Marge Simms, in establishing a testimony for the Lord in that area.

Nearly all the villages for miles around knew of the miraculous change in the chief's life as well as the lives of many of the people in his village. All knew the story of Chief Paul's elderly mother, Bio, who had been revealed as the adopted mother of a French-African by the name of Martin Blanc. Martin had appeared on the scene, keeping his identity with Bio a secret. Bio had been marvelously saved. Just before she died of a heart attack, the old woman revealed the secret which, by tribal law, made Chief Paul and Martin brothers.

It was Martin's assignment from his Communist superiors to penetrate his Banda tribe and establish a worker's union among them. Upon his arrival, however, he had met with unexpected opposition from missionaries Ken and Marge Simms. Ken and Marge had moved to the mission station, Yanga Two, to replace Paul and Becky Davis. The Davises had returned to the States due to Becky's sudden illness. One week after their arrival in the States, Becky had died.

It was not unusual for Chief Paul to spend several days at a time at Yanga Two with his beloved missionaries. They often recounted the days of Martin Blanc's time among them and the way God took something evil and turned it into a testimony for Himself. The fact that the missionaries had to constantly use a foreign language didn't seem to limit their fellowship with the African believers.

The dry season sun had reached its peak in the cloudless sky. Chief Paul and Ken were sitting on the front veranda, chatting.

"What do you hear from Mr. Davis, Dr. Simms?" asked the chief.

"I just received a letter from him in the last mail," replied the medical doctor. "Excuse me just a moment, Chief Paul, and I'll get it."

While Ken went for the letter, the village chief smiled as he looked out over the mission compound. Even though many months had passed, it seemed only recently that it had all happened. Seriously ill with malaria, the chief had been brought by the missionaries to the mission station to be treated. He recalled watching the mob from his village, led by his brother Kota, as they came to "rescue" him from the "evil missionaries."

"After all," Kota had said to the people at the village of Yanga One, "if we don't rescue my brother, those white men will kill him."

The smile faded from the chief's face as he remembered the spear thrown by Tene, one of the young men from his village. The spear had gone through the bedroom window where Paul and Becky Davis were lying in bed. Fortunately, it had passed harmlessly over them, striking against the far wall.

"Here it is," said Ken, returning to his friend. "Let's see now, it was written just fourteen days ago." He began reading the letter.

" 'I made a trip to the mission's home office and shared with the staff that I would like to return in six months. As we talked, they encouraged me to return as soon as I feel ready. My heart is with my dear friends in Africa and I hope to return within a few weeks. Thank you for sending me the list of the things you need. I'll do my best to get it all for you. When you see Chief Paul, tell him that I'm praying daily for him and his people. I am often reminded of the wonderful miracles that God did not only in Chief Paul's life, but also in the lives of many in that whole area.'

" 'I received a letter from Martin and Marie this last week.

Thank you for sending me their address. It seems as if I've known them for years, even though I've never met them. They write that they would like to enter Bible school this fall and asked me what I thought of them learning English and taking their Bible training here in the United States. I wrote them two days ago telling them I thought it would be best for them to enroll in the mission's new Bible school there in France. I'm sure they will do that. We must pray for them. For some reason, I felt that Martin wanted to leave France as soon as possible. I'm sure he will write you concerning this matter.' "

"There's something wrong with Martin and Marie," spoke up Chief Paul. "I know my people well enough to know that all is not well."

Ken studied the look on the African's face. This was one of the areas of the local culture he did not understand. Africans seemed to read each other very well. It was nearly impossible for any one of them to hide his or her feelings.

"What makes you say that, Chief?" asked Ken. "You seem to speak with absolute assurance."

"I'm sure, Dr. Simms!" replied the village chief. "I can tell by Martin's letter to Mr. Davis that something is wrong. We may not find out right away what it is, but we probably will hear about it sometime in the future. Things like that have a way of surfacing."

Ken knew that Chief Paul spoke with authority when speaking about his people—and Martin Blanc was still one of his people, even though he was half French.

"That's good news about Mr. Davis coming back and with all those medical supplies, too. I can hardly wait until Martin and Marie finish their Bible school training. We need them at Yanga One. But until then, you and Mrs. Simms can operate our dispensary; right, Dr. Simms?"

"You're right, Chief Paul," laughed the American doctor, reaching out to shake the hand of his African friend. "Even if it is on a part-time basis. By the way, Chief, we're going to have something very special for dinner tonight. We bought them at the capital our last trip there. We have been saving them for a very special friend and there's no better time to eat them than while you're with us."

Ken's remarks stirred the African's curiosity. He gave Ken a puzzled look. "Tell me what it is, Dr. Simms."

"Well, since you asked me, I will." A smile spread across the missionary's face as he looked at his friend. "Tonight we are going to eat hot dogs!"

It took a few seconds for the words to make their impact on the chief.

"Hot dogs?" replied the surprised African. "Dr. Simms, did I hear you say hot dogs?" The chief reached out his long arm and snapped his fingers with a loud crack. Then he held his hand to his mouth. The expression on his face was sheer amazement and disbelief. Ken tried to keep from laughing as he watched the village chief. Again, the African snapped his fingers.

"Dr. Simms, your words have completely taken me by surprise. My mind does not know what to think. There may be nothing wrong with eating dogs, but it does seem strange for you people to eat them. Not even everyone in our tribe will eat them. You will find some of the very old men who will, but it must be a dog that has gone mad. They will not eat a dog that did not have a bad sickness."

"I'm sorry I surprised you so much, Chief Paul," said Ken, not wanting to reveal his joke. "Mrs. Simms is in the kitchen getting things ready for the meal. Do you want to watch her?"

"No, thank you, Dr. Simms. I'll wait until I see it on the table. I must tell you, however, that it will be the first time I have eaten a dog."

The two men walked out toward the dispensary. In his visits to the mission station, Chief Paul always wanted to see the room where he was saved. He never ceased to marvel at what God did for him on that first visit to the mission station.

"That's the place, right there," said Chief Paul, pointing to the spot where he had made his decision. "That's where I was when Jesus became my Savior—and you were the one who helped me."

The two men stood talking about the many things that had happened since Chief Paul's conversion. As they talked, Marge called them for dinner.

"Come and get it! Dinner is ready!"

The African chief was always ready and anxious to eat with his missionary friends. This time, however, he seemed a bit hesitant.

He looked around as he entered the house, wondering if he would catch a glimpse of the "hot dogs." The three sat down and Ken prayed, thanking the Lord for the food.

Marge lifted the metal lid off the tray where the steaming frankfurters lay. Their African friend carefully studied the strange-looking objects before him.

"Well, there they are, Chief Paul," said Ken, smiling. "There are the hot dogs."

"But that doesn't look like dog meat to me," answered the guest.

"Oh, they aren't the kind of dogs you're thinking of, Chief Paul. These are made from beef. We just call them hot dogs in our country," responded Ken. "Here, try one." The missionary doctor handed the tray to the chief, who took it and began to laugh.

"And I thought you were going to make me eat dog meat." He carefully speared two of the frankfurters with his fork and placed them on his plate. Slowly he cut a piece off one of them and put it in his mouth. "I like the hot dogs, Dr. Simms. They don't bark, do they?" said the happy chief.

They all looked at each other and laughed. Ken could not help but think of the man Chief Paul had been before he was saved. Second Corinthians 5:17 ran through his mind. Truly their African friend had experienced the joy of old things passing away and all things becoming new. After the meal, the three friends sat in the front room talking.

"I want to invite you to a special meal at my house," said Chief Paul. "I want you to enjoy my speciality."

"What's that?" asked Marge.

"Manioc dipped in caterpillar sauce," answered the chief. "I don't know whether I should invite you now or wait until Mr. Davis returns."

"Why don't you wait until Mr. Davis returns?" suggested Ken, looking somewhat pale.

"I think that's a good idea," added Marge. "Let's wait until Mr. Davis is here. I'm sure he would want to be in on such a special treat."

Ken stood up and excused himself. "I think I should take a look at my patients. Besides, I like the freshness of the night air here in Africa."

Marge smiled to herself. She knew Ken wanted to change the conversation, and his patients provided the best excuse.

Chief Paul was also aware of what was going on. In his heart, he felt content. He, too, knew how to play this game. That night in his room, the African leader chuckled as he thought of the look on Ken's face.

3
Strange Turn of Events

Martin's heart beat wildly as he opened the apartment door. There, standing in the hallway, was a familiar face—the same man who had been coming to the clothing store the past few weeks to talk to him about rejoining the Party.

"Hello, Martin," said the visitor. "I've come to speak to you and Marie. It is very important, so I would suggest you invite me in."

"I've told you before that we'll have nothing to do with the Party. Please leave us alone!" Martin's voice carried a tone of finality. "Marie and I have accepted Christ as our Savior and we do not believe in the doctrines of communism any more."

"You've told me that before, Martin," said the Communist agent, "but I don't understand what you're saying."

Martin sensed his visitor was sincere and really did want to know what was meant by accepting Christ. The French-African Christian stepped aside and motioned for the man in the hall to enter.

"Please do sit down," said Martin, pointing to a chair. "I'll call Marie."

As she entered the room, Marie looked at their visitor, who was rising to his feet. Her eyes widened in surprise.

"Why, hello, Mr. Duval," she said, offering her hand.

"Hello, Marie," replied the Party worker. "How are you?"

"Do . . . do you know each other?" asked Martin, somewhat bewildered.

"Yes, we do," responded the man, half smiling. "I know

Marie's parents. I stayed in their home several times. Marie was in her teens when I visited them. Now, tell me, Martin, what is this that you told me about you and Marie not wanting to be in the Party any more—that you both have accepted Christ as your . . . your . . . how do you say it? Savior?"

"We are aware that you know a lot about us, Mr. Duval. I was with the Party long enough to know that. When the Party assigned me to Central Africa to penetrate my people, the Banda tribe, I went without hesitation. I didn't realize, however, that I was going to meet up with some opposition from American missionaries."

"American missionaries?" repeated the visitor.

"Yes," responded Martin. "I was very rough on them, thinking they would get discouraged and leave. Instead of treating me the same way, they showed me love. They treated my leg, which was badly ulcerated."

"They really did that?" questioned the agent. There was a flicker of interest in his eyes.

"They did. I just couldn't understand at the time why they were so kind to me."

"Evidently you do now," suggested the Frenchman.

"We do, Mr. Duval! Marie and I really do understand why our American missionary friends did what they did."

"Tell me about it, Martin, if you will. There is something here which I don't understand and which I want to know. You and Marie are just too serious about all of this for it not to be very important to you."

Martin then told in detail how he tried to create a worker's union. He spoke of Chief Paul and his cooperation at first. He also related the story of his stepmother Bio, Chief Paul's mother. "At the time of my mother's death, she gave me to Bio. This was a secret known only to Bio and me later on," said Martin.

"That meant you and this chief were brothers," added the visitor.

"You are correct. My father took me immediately after my mother died and raised me. I can't go into all the details, but I caused a church building to be burned one night. An African pastor was caught in the fire trying to rescue the casket and body of my stepmother. She had died that day of a heart attack, but I didn't know her body was in the church when I set the fire. I really didn't intend to hurt anyone. The pastor was badly burned, but he sent for me to come. Like the missionaries, he spoke to me about Jesus, God's Son. It was then that I began to see my horrible self. He told me how the Bible, God's Word, reveals that all men are sinners; and that the result of sin is eternal death. I was told how Jesus came to earth and died for the sins of the world, including my sins."

"I've never heard anything like this before," said the Communist agent.

"Neither had I," answered Martin. "But when I saw the love and concern of those missionaries and the change in the lives of my people who had accepted Christ, I knew they had something that was real. It was a supernatural work in their lives. It was all so very foreign to me."

"That's wonderful," interrupted the visitor.

"It is wonderful," agreed Martin. "I, too, accepted Christ as my Savior by confessing my sins to God and asking Him to save me and make me His child."

"And He did it, didn't He, Martin?" asked the agent.

"Yes, He did do it—and not only for me, but for Marie, too. We are both Christians, Mr. Duval. Christ is our Savior and Heaven is our eternal Home." Martin noticed the sadness in their visitor's eyes. Marie sat silently nearby, praying for Mr. Duval.

"That is why we left the Party, Mr. Duval. Communism is anti-God. It is atheistic. You can see why we can't have anything to do with it."

"Yes, I can see, Martin. I really can."

"Mr. Duval," spoke Marie, "why don't you accept Jesus as your Savior? He died for you, too. He'll save you from your sins and give you everlasting life. Wouldn't you like to accept Him?"

The look on the agent's face indicated the struggle in his heart. He searched for the words as he spoke. "I understand what you are saying, Marie. I guess I'm not as brave as you and Martin. I'm afraid of what would happen to me and my family if I would do as you have done. I'm sorry, but . . . but I can't do it."

Mr. Duval stood and walked toward the door. "I must go now. You won't be hearing from the Party any more. I'll personally see to that. And . . . and . . . don't worry about me. I'll be all right."

The agent held out his hand. "Good-bye, Marie. Good-bye, Martin. Thank you for sharing these things with me. I'm happy for both of you."

The door closed behind the Frenchman, leaving two thankful but sad Christians on the other side; thankful for the visit and the opportunity to witness for the Lord, but saddened and burdened for Mr. Duval, who was still lost and without Christ. Martin and Marie immediately slipped to their knees to pray for their unusual visitor.

4
Come Back, Mr. Duval

The traffic on Oakland Avenue was heavier than usual. Paul Davis never had enjoyed driving in the city. The many road construction projects made the driving on this trip even more undesirable. As he headed down the highway leading from the city, his heart was filled with praise. His meeting with the mission's executive staff had turned out far better than he could have hoped.

"Thank You, Father, for those dear friends in the home office," he prayed audibly as he drove along. Paul had just learned that a large sum of money had been given to him for the new work at Yanga One. Besides that, there was a large, unexpected supply of medicine and medical equipment which had been given to the mission for any special needs. The home office staff decided that Yanga One would be the logical place to send the medical supplies.

The trip home was a pleasant one for Paul. Five hours after leaving the mission's headquarters, the missionary pulled into his driveway, parked his car, and went to the mailbox to pick up the past week's mail. His eyes caught the familiar blue envelope with the beautiful butterfly stamps on it.

"A letter from Ken and Marge," he whispered to himself. "Wonder what they have to say?" Paul quickly tore open the envelope and pulled out the onionskin paper. He read carefully.

"Chief Paul was with us two weeks ago. He stayed for three days. What a blessing he has been to us. Of course, we talked about his sickness and how you and I brought him to the mission station to treat him. He never gets tired of talking about that experience."

Paul stopped reading a moment to think of that night when the chief's brother, Kota, had led a group of men from Yanga One to attack the mission station and "rescue" Kota's brother. He thought of the spear that came through their bedroom window, just passing over their heads. A chill ran up his spine. Paul's eyes moistened as he thought of Becky's sudden illness and her death shortly after they returned to the States. The words on the letter blurred as he wiped away the tears.

"I shared with Chief Paul your letter telling that Martin and Marie want to train in America. He declared that Martin and Marie were facing some kind of problem and wanted to run from it. Being one who knows his people well, he must be correct. It will be interesting to see what develops."

Paul read through the rest of the letter and then looked at the remaining mail. Near the bottom of the stack was a letter from Martin and Marie Blanc. Excitedly, he opened the envelope.

"We have good news for you," he read. "The Lord has worked things out so that we no longer want to come to America to study. We will be applying here in the new Bible college."

Paul then read on as Martin described the visit of the Communist agent, Mr. Duval, and the circumstances leading up to the visit. He was careful to relate how he and Marie had opportunity to witness to their visitor.

"Our hearts were heavy when he left us. We know he recognized his need for Christ, but he is afraid of what may happen to him and his family. Please pray for him. He said he would see to it that the Party would not bother us again. I don't know what he plans to do; but I do know that if the Party ever finds out he is shielding us, it will be hard on him."

Standing beside the mailbox, Paul bowed his head and prayed for Mr. Duval. Wouldn't it be something, he thought, if Martin and Marie had the joy of leading the agent to the Lord. Paul made his way to the house with the two important letters.

Dan and Alice Fine, missionaries in Paris, had tried to be as much help and encouragement as possible to the two former Communist agents, Marie and Martin Blanc. The couple made it a point to visit with Martin and Marie at least once each week. They saw each other on Sundays and at midweek prayer meetings, but there was little time for any private conversation at those times.

It was Marie's birthday and Alice had baked a large birthday cake for her. For the occasion, Dr. and Mrs. deCharles, a French-American couple, were invited. Dr. deCharles was director of the new Bible college. Dan thought it would be an excellent opportunity for the two couples to get to know each other.

"I understand you both are former Communists," said the theologian to Martin and Marie.

Martin hesitated to answer, sensing there was another question to follow. "Yes . . . yes . . . we are former Communists. God brought some wonderful people into our lives—people who not only know God but love Him. Someday I would love to write a book on the many wonderful things God has done for Marie and me." Martin went on to share the recent incident concerning Mr. Duval.

"The reason I refer to your past lives is that I, too, have had extensive exposure to communism," continued Dr. deCharles.

"You have?" spoke Martin, with an air of excitement. "Where did that take place?"

"I have been arrested a number of times by Communist government police," responded the professor. "During my contacts with the Communists, I came to know several of them quite well. What is Mr. Duval's first name, Marie? Could it be Henry?"

"Yes," replied Marie, excitedly, "it is Henry. I remember my father calling him by that name."

"Actually, he goes by at least two names," said Dr. deCharles. "I've also heard him called Raymond Bouvier, but that was behind the Iron Curtain. He is definitely a strong link between Moscow and the French-Communist Party. It is strange that you had never met him before, Martin. I know there's a reason for it. They have a reason for everything."

Martin wanted to ask the college director if he had received their application papers. He was relieved when Dr. deCharles changed the conversation from their past to their applications.

"By the way, our application committee looked over your applications this past week. Everything looks good. I'm sure the recommendation letter for you, Martin, will be in shortly. Dr. Simms is very prompt with his correspondence. As it looks now, you folks will be able to enter school this fall."

Martin shivered with excitement. "That's wonderful news, Dr. deCharles. Marie and I are looking forward to this time of preparation. Whatever He wants for us is what we want." The French-African choked up, and tears appeared in his eyes. "I guess my heart is pretty tender, Dr. deCharles. It doesn't seem possible that this has all happened. Thank the Lord for Pastor Kondo and Chief Paul and Dr. Simms. God used all of them to bring me to Himself."

The room was silent as Martin took out his handkerchief and wiped his eyes. Marie reached over and touched him on the arm.

"Just think," Martin said, smiling through the tears, "from communism to Christ. What a miracle. What a testimony of God's love and grace."

"That's right, Martin," spoke up Dan Fine. "There aren't too many Communist agents who get saved, let alone go to Bible school."

"Speaking of Communist agents," inserted Dr. deCharles, "let's focus our prayers on Henry Duval. Let's ask God to bring him back into our lives. He seems too interested for us to allow him simply to slip away."

Later that night in their apartment, Martin and Marie spoke of their conversation at the home of Dan and Alice Fine.

"How can we make contact with Mr. Duval, Martin?" asked Marie. "We don't want to be careless and put him under suspicion."

"I'm sure the Lord will direct us in our efforts to reach him," responded Martin. "He knows where he is and He can work it all out for us."

"Isn't it amazing to see how the whole picture has changed?" Marie laughed. "A short time ago we were anxious to leave France to get away from Mr. Duval. Now, we're asking God to bring him back into our lives."

"That's the Lord, honey," said Martin. "Remember, He says in His Word, 'For my thoughts are not your thoughts, neither are your ways my ways.'"

"I'm so glad our lives are controlled by Him, Martin," spoke Marie, squeezing her husband's hand.

"Happy birthday, Marie," responded Martin, smiling.

5
Paul Returns

"Tomorrow we'll be in Douala, Rev. Davis." The young missionary looked up from his position beside the rail to see the ship's captain approaching.

"It's been a pleasant two weeks, Captain Stine. You and your crew have made me feel like a part of your ship's family."

"Thank you," responded the captain. "We've enjoyed having you on board. I especially enjoyed all our interesting conversations. Another week and I think you might have converted me."

The captain smiled as he spoke. His words were more in jest than anything else. He had a healthy respect for Paul as a Christian and had often told him so throughout the trip across the Atlantic. The first day out of Baltimore, Paul had opportunity to share his faith with the veteran seaman who introduced himself to the three passengers on the middle-sized freighter.

"I've enjoyed talking with you, Captain Stine. Your questions have been very probing and I'll always remember our times together." Paul paused for a moment and then continued. "As I mentioned to you yesterday, you can accept Christ as your Savior at any time or any place. Remember that verse in the book of Romans that I read to you so many times?"

"How can I ever forget it?" laughed the captain. "Now let's see. 'If thou shalt confess with thy mouth the Lord Jesus, and shalt believe in thine heart that God hath raised him from the dead, thou shalt be saved.'"

"Great!" Paul called out enthusiastically. "That's just great! I couldn't do any better myself." Paul put his hand on the captain's shoulder. "You quoted that verse so beautifully, Captain Stine. Let me ask you now, do you believe what you said?"

The captain glanced at the deck and then at Paul. "I know what it says, Rev. Davis. I understand it very well, but I'm not ready to accept Christ as my Savior. I must give it more thought."

The two men shook hands and the captain returned to the bridge. Paul returned to his cabin to get some rest. One more day and he would be starting the 1400-mile trip inland.

The bright morning sun beat down on the African dockworkers. Paul had arrived on deck from the dining room just in time to see his light blue pickup truck being lifted out of the hold of the ship. Slowly the huge boom swung out over the side of the freighter, carrying the truck like a toy. Gradually it let the truck down until its wheels gently touched the dock. Paul felt good inside knowing that his truck was finally on African soil.

"There it is, ready to roll," came a voice behind the missionary. Captain Stine reached out to shake Paul's hand. "I'd better say good-bye now, Rev. Davis. I have to get back up to the bridge, but I wanted to see you before you left the ship."

"Thank you, Captain Stine," said Paul. "It's been a wonderful trip. I've enjoyed every moment of it, and our times together made it that much more enjoyable. I . . . I am going to continue to pray for you that one of these days you will accept Christ as your Savior."

"Thank you, Rev. Davis. I may surprise you by doing that. I have your address. You may be sure that I will write you if I do."

The two friends shook hands and parted. Paul's heart was heavy for the captain, but yet there was that glimmer of hope that the seaman knew the gospel and understood what he had to do to be saved.

The trip inland was a lonely one for Paul. Since there were very few places along the way where he could buy gasoline, he carried two 55-gallon drums of fuel in the back of the truck. Whenever the tank got low, he would stop, take an eight-foot plastic hose and siphon the gas into the tank, passing it through a chamois spread across a large-mouth funnel. This kept out any water or dirt, which was found in gas stored in barrels.

"I'll be glad to get back," said Paul to himself as he made his way inland. "It will be good to see all my friends again."

Because of the deep ruts and large stones in the road, good traveling time was out of the question. Paul was forced to leave the road in places and travel on the nearby grassy plains until he could get back on the road. The case of bottled spring water he bought at the coast was nearly gone when the blue pickup arrived at the city limits of the capital of the landlocked Central African country. Once he passed the city limits' road barrier checkpoint, Paul was able to travel on the blacktop road. The small pickup purred along the hard surface. Within ten minutes from the time he left the barrier, he drove into the mission station driveway. Dale Banks spotted the blue pickup as soon as it arrived. Within minutes the two men were shaking hands.

"It's great to have you back, Paul," said Dale. "And you look so good. Furlough must have agreed with you."

"It is great to be back, Dale. I must admit it's a lot different without Becky, but the Lord has really helped me this past year."

"Hi, Paul, welcome back." Dale and Paul turned to see Dorothy Banks coming out the front door. "You sure are a sight for sore eyes," said the young missionary wife, shaking Paul's hand.

Paul looked around as the three friends entered the house. "Hey, you've painted the place!" exlaimed Paul. "It's beautiful. You made a good choice of colors."

"Dorothy chose them," Dale said proudly. "She's the interior decorator in our house. By the way, Paul," he continued with a slight grin on his face, "do you happen to know a lady by the name of Ann Steele?"

"No, I don't know anyone by that name. Why do you ask?"

"Well, Ken and Marge were down two weeks ago. While here, they went to pick up their mail before it was sent up-country. In it was a letter from a nurse who lives in Indianapolis. She asked if she could come and work out here for two or three months."

"That's tremendous!" interrupted Paul. "Maybe she can help Marge set up the new dispensary at Yanga One."

"The reason I asked if you knew her, Paul, is because you have a letter from her, too. It came yesterday." Dale handed the letter to his co-worker, who stuck his finger under the corner of the flap and tore it open. Slowly he pulled out the neatly folded letter. The more he read, the more excited he became.

"Dale! Dorothy! Listen to this." Paul began reading the letter.

" 'Dear Rev. Davis, I'm sure this will be a surprise to you to hear from me. We have never met each other personally, but I know who you are because you spoke at my home church in Indianapolis. The morning I heard you, you told of your work there in Africa. I clearly recall how you described the attack on the mission station and the conversion of an African chief. My heart was deeply touched when you told of the death of Mrs. Davis. As you spoke, I kept wondering if there were some way I could help in the medical work for a summer.

" 'My pastor gave me your mission's home office address. I wrote and received the address of Dr. and Mrs. Simms and also the address of Rev. and Mrs. Banks. I was told that you would stop off at their house on your way inland.' "

Paul stopped to comment. "This is terrific. We never know what the Lord is doing in hearts when we speak."

"How true," said Dale. "It sure is a blessing to hear of results like this."

Paul continued with the letter. " 'I have written to Dr. and Mrs. Simms and asked them if they can use me this coming summer. Since you are the one through whom the Lord spoke to my heart about the needs there, I wanted to share this with you as well. I am twenty-seven years old and a widow. My husband, Tom, and our only child, two-year-old David, were killed in an automobile accident two years ago.' "

Paul hesitated a moment. Dale and Dorothy sat in silence as he read on. They knew the letter had touched his heart.

" 'I understand the mission will be writing to you missionaries to see if I can come out this summer. If there are any suggestions from any of you to help me prepare for this trip and ministry, please do let me know. I'll be praying for each of you by name.' "

"I hardly know what to say," said Paul, placing the letter back into the envelope. "Who knows? Maybe Mrs. Steele is another missionary for this country."

That night before retiring in the guest bedroom, Paul read Ann Steele's letter again. He had an indescribable feeling as he prayed for Ann. Somehow he felt that she was heading for a life in missions and, if so, he wanted to do all he could to help her.

6
Wedding News

The capital city showed little change from the city that Paul Davis had left months before. The Palace Restaurant with its French cuisine was still the attraction to the white foreign population. Paul's thoughts turned to Becky as he drove by the restaurant one afternoon while doing some shopping for up-country supplies. He recalled that they had gone there for a meal every time they came down to the capital. It had always been a special treat to which Becky had looked forward.

It was nearly five o'clock when Paul started back to the mission station. Dale Banks was doing some repair work on his car when Paul arrived at the station.

"I'm glad to see you are still working, Dale. I thought I was late for dinner."

"No problem, Paul." Dale poked his head out from underneath the car. "Since there are no guests other than yourself, Dorothy and I thought we would take you out to dinner tonight at the Palace."

"That would be nice," reponded Paul. "I've really missed that cordon bleu. I think it's the best French dish. I've never found a restaurant in America that could make it like these French cooks."

In spite of the memories the Palace brought back, Paul enjoyed the evening with his co-workers. He joked with several of the waiters whom he knew. When one of them asked about his wife, he told of her death.

Early the next morning, Paul headed up-country with his

loaded pickup. The missionaries all had an understanding that anyone going up-country from the capital would transport supplies for the missionaries along the way. Ken Simms had sent a telegram asking Paul to bring ten bags of cement for Yanga Two.

Because of the rough road conditions, travel was slow. Paul didn't arrive at the Bible school station until nine o'clock that evening.

"Hello, Paul, welcome back!" called Bill Dykes from the front door as Paul brought the pickup to a stop. The headlights of the truck told the Bible school students that someone had arrived. Within minutes the path between the mission station and the Bible school village was filled with men, women and children on their way to see the visitor.

"It's Mr. Davis!" called one of the students. "He's arrived!" Tene, the student from Yanga One, felt his heart skip with excitement when he heard the name of his missionary friend.

"Mr. Davis," he repeated. "Thank You, Lord, for bringing him back." The young student pushed into the group of people who surrounded Paul. Hands were reaching out everywhere to touch their beloved missionary and to shake his hand.

"Hello, Mr. Davis!" called Tene, his voice filled with emotion. "It's me—Tene."

"Hello, Tene," called Paul, reaching out to hug the African.

"How are you? It's good to see you. I'm so glad you are back," said Tene, trying hard to hold back the tears. "My heart ached much for you, Mr. Davis. I know the death of Mrs. Davis must have caused you great pain."

"It did, Tene," said Paul, "but the Lord's strength was there through it all."

The rest of the Africans listened as Paul and Tene spoke with each other. They knew of the incident at Yanga Two when Tene, before his conversion, had thrown a spear through the bedroom window, just missing Paul and Becky.

"Isn't it wonderful to know, Mr. Davis, that God never makes a mistake with things that come into our lives?" Tene's spiritual maturity surprised Paul. His heart was thrilled to see such growth in the young man.

Paul was tired from his all-day trip and went to bed not long after he entered the house. Bill and Kathy Dykes insisted that he get some rest. "We'll catch up on the news tomorrow," said Bill as he bid Paul good night.

As hard as he tried, Paul could not get to sleep. It seemed as if he missed Becky far more in Africa than he did in America. He reached over and touched the side of the bed where she had often slept during their stopovers at the Bible school station.

"Father," prayed Paul softly, "I know You never make a mistake. I must confess, however, that there are some things I don't understand. And, Lord, one of them is Becky's Homegoing. She was such a sweet girl, Father. You know how I loved her. Now she's in Heaven with You." The hot tears ran from Paul's eyes. "Father, I miss her so very much. Help me to bear this burden. I'm not asking You to take it away. Just help me to bear it."

As Paul wiped the tears from his eyes, Romans 8:28 came to mind. Slowly he quoted it. "And we know that all things work together for good to them that love God, to them who are the called according to his purpose." A smile spread across Paul's face. "Thank You, Lord. Thank You for including 'all things' in that verse."

The rising sun cast a sliver of light across the room like a miniature highway. The beam finally focused on Paul's face. The sleeping missionary frowned, squinted his eyes, and then slowly opened them. He looked at his watch.

"Oh, no!" he cried, jumping out of bed. "It's seven-thirty and Kathy always has breakfast at seven." He quickly dressed and made his way to the dining room. There he found Kathy studying for her Bible class.

"I'm sorry, Kathy. I never sleep this late," exclaimed Paul apologetically.

"Don't think anything of it, Paul," responded the young housewife. "Bill and I decided we would eat when you got up. We knew you were tired, and right now your rest is very important. I'll call Bill. He's talking to a couple of the students out front."

The Bible school station had an abundance of fruit trees. Whenever missionaries left, they always had a good supply of fruit to take with them. Those on the station enjoyed the fruit also, and Kathy knew just how to blend the fruits together.

"These bananas are so delicious," said Paul, filling up his bowl for the third time. "Do you mind, Kathy?"

"Not at all, Paul. It does my heart good to see people eat at our table."

"Well, it's not hard to do, Kathy," exclaimed Paul. "By the way, have you folks heard about the short-termer who wants to come out?"

"Haven't heard a thing," answered Bill. "Tell us about him."

"Well, to begin with, he happens to be a woman. In fact, she's a widow and a nurse. She has written Ken and Marge to see if they can use her at Yanga One and Yanga Two."

"What's her name, Paul?" questioned Kathy.

"Her name is Ann Steele. She's from Indianapolis."

"Do you know her?" asked Bill.

"No, I don't. She wrote me at the capital and told me about her desire to come and help. She said that the Lord first spoke to her heart when she heard me speak in her home church. She sounds like a real nice girl. Her husband and young son were killed in an automobile accident two years ago." Suddenly Paul felt a bit awkward as he spoke about Ann Steele. Kathy noticed his uneasiness and changed the subject.

"Why don't you stay with us for a few days, Paul? We would love to have you here. I promise to give you fruit every meal if you stay."

"You sure know my weakness, Kathy," Paul responded laughing. "I really think, though, that I should be on my way today." A sad look appeared on his face. "I guess I miss Becky more than I ever thought I would. It is really lonely without her."

Paul's co-workers sat in silent understanding. A few moments later the sound of the clearing of a throat was heard on the front porch.

"There's someone outside to see you, Paul," spoke Bill, glancing out the window. "It looks like someone wants to send some fruit for his family."

Outside in the driveway stood Tene. Beside him was a large stalk of bananas and three baskets of grapefruit and oranges.

"No doubt some of it is going to his future in-laws," continued Bill. "Did you know that Tene plans to get married next year?"

"Who is the fortunate girl?" inquired Paul as he moved toward the front door.

"Pastor's Kondo's daughter, Ruth. Chief Paul and the pastor have already made all the arrangements for the wedding."

"Just think," said Paul, stopping at the door to speak to his co-workers, "wedding bells at Yanga One, or . . . or will it be at Yanga Two? Well, at any rate, there will be wedding bells at one of them."

As Paul stepped out into the driveway, little did he realize what a tremendous change in his life those wedding bells would bring.

7
Caterpillar Sauce

The sound of the truck horn brought the villagers running to the mission station at Yanga Two.

"Mr. Davis is back!" shouted one of the men to Pastor Kondo, pastor of the church in Yanga Two. The African pastor had been digging yams in back of the village. He stuck his hand hoe underneath some of the yam vines and headed for the mission compound.

The blue pickup turned down the long driveway leading to the back of the station where the mission house was located. By the time it reached the end of the driveway, the Africans had it surrounded. A sea of happy faces brought tears to Paul's eyes.

"Welcome back, Mr. Davis," called one of the men, reaching into the cab to shake Paul's hand.

"You have returned," said another, clapping his hands.

The press of people made it difficult for Paul to get the door open, but he finally managed and stepped out onto the ground. Before he realized what was happening, one of the older women of the village walked up to him, took his head in her hands, and gently blew into his ear.

"Thank you, Mama," said Paul, squeezing her hand. The missionary knew that such a greeting from a Banda tribesman or woman was very special and rarely done.

"Hello, Paul!" called a familiar voice. Paul turned to see his co-worker, Ken Simms, coming from the dispensary.

"Hi, Ken. What a welcome! I sure never expected this." The

Africans made an opening for Ken to reach his fellow missionary. The missionary doctor put his arms around Paul.

"It's so good to see you, Paul. Marge and I have prayed daily for you."

"Welcome home, Paul," called Marge, coming hurriedly from the house. "We've been waiting for this moment a long time."

After shaking hands with his co-workers, Paul continued to greet the Africans who came to welcome him. A number had run back to the village and were returning with chickens and eggs. One even brought a goat. Their missionary had returned and nothing was too good for him.

About an hour after his arrival, Paul made his way into the house with Ken and Marge. As he entered the front room, a strange feeling ran through him. It seemed that only days had passed since his dear wife had suffered from the fatal cancer. He walked to the bedroom and looked in. The bed was still in the same place. It was there that Ken Simms had examined Becky and decided to send her to the hospital at the capital. Sensing that Paul was thinking about those last days at Yanga Two, Ken and Marge stood silently by, waiting for their friend to speak. A smile appeared on Paul's face as he pointed to the far corner of the bedroom.

"Don't tell me that Tẹne's spear is still here?"

"It's still there, Paul," grinned Ken. "You left it there, and for some reason Marge and I just didn't have the heart to move it. After all, it is a very valuable reminder of the battle for Yanga One."

"You are so right, Ken," responded Paul. "I'll never forget the night it came flying through that screened window over there. Becky and I just happened to be low enough for it to pass over our heads. It hit there against the wall. In fact, there's the mark."

"Paul," spoke Ken, "I told Chief Paul that as soon as you arrived, I would let him know. I'm sure he will want to come and stay a few days. Maybe I should go now so I can get back before dark."

"Don't you think I should ride along with you, Ken?" asked Paul. "It will only take a couple of hours."

"You've traveled enough today, Paul. Why don't you get your truck unloaded? By that time, Marge will have something for you to eat. Besides, I'm sure you will want to shower and get some of that red dirt off you."

Ken made the twenty-mile trip to Yanga One in good time. Chief Paul was sitting out in front of his large house in his favorite chaise lounge. He rose quickly when he saw the pickup truck enter his village.

"Hello, Dr. Simms," he called, walking over to greet his American friend. "What good news brings you here today?"

"You must be a mind reader, Chief Paul," responded Ken. "I do have good news."

"Don't tell me," said the chief quickly. "Let me tell you what the good news is you've brought me." Ken sensed the Christian chief was in an exceptionally jolly mood.

"All right, my friend, tell me."

Looking at Ken with a big grin, Chief Paul spoke loudly, clearly enunciating each word. "You–came–to–tell–me–that–our–good–brother–Mr.–Davis–has–arrived."

"You're right," said Ken, laughing. "And now you're going to tell me that you want to go back with me to Yanga Two to stay for a few days."

"And you're right, Dr. Simms. I'll have my things ready in a short time." In twenty minutes Chief Paul's suitcase was in the back of the pickup. He also had his men tie several goats in the truck.

"The goats are for Mr. Davis. I'm taking my cook along this time, Dr. Simms. I will need him."

The return trip to the mission station took a bit longer than Ken had anticipated. Chief Paul wanted to take Paul Davis the biggest rooster he could find. Just when he thought he had purchased the chicken he wanted, he would spot another one a little larger. When they arrived at the mission station, there were five roosters and three goats in the back of the truck.

Paul was out in the driveway when the pickup came to a stop. He opened the door for his African friend. "Hello, Chief Paul. How are you?"

"I'm fine, Mr. Davis," responded the chief, stepping down to the ground. "How are you?"

The two men faced each other, shaking hands as they spoke. Suddenly Paul Davis felt like he was really back home. Before him was one of his dearest friends.

Knowing that Paul was tired, everyone retired early. Before he went to bed, Chief Paul went out to the truck and brought in a covered basket. For some reason unknown to his missionary friends, he wanted to keep it in his bedroom.

The next morning Paul Davis was sitting in the front room reading when Ken came out of the bedroom.

"Good morning, Paul," said Ken. "Did you sleep well last night?"

"Slept real well, Ken," answered Paul. He hesitated a moment and spoke again. "I don't know if you have noticed, but there is a strange smell by the guest rooms. It seemed to become stronger through the night. It's really quite bad in there, Ken."

"Now that you mention it, I do smell something. I thought it might be one of those trees in the forest with the bad-smelling seed pods. They have a smell something like this." Ken went to the open screened window and took a long, deep breath. "Well, I can tell you, it isn't out there. It's definitely in the house."

"I wonder if it could be a dead lizzard or rat," suggested Paul.

Ken raised his eyebrows as he spoke. "Could be. Maybe we should make a search after breakfast."

The door leading into the guest end hallway opened and Chief Paul stepped out with a big smile. "Good morning, Mr. Davis. Good morning, Dr. Simms. How are you men this beautiful morning?" With the door open, an even stronger odor penetrated the room.

"We are fine, thank you, Chief Paul," responded Ken. "And how is our dear friend, Chief Paul, this morning?"

"I'm fine, too. I've really been looking forward to this day for a long time—a long time."

"Tell me, Chief," continued Ken, "do you smell something? Mr. Davis thinks that maybe a lizzard or a rat died near the guest rooms."

"I don't smell anything bad, Dr. Simms. I'm sure if there was anything dead in there, I'd smell it."

Ken decided to end that conversation for the time being. "By the way, Chief Paul, my wife and I have decided to take you and Mr. Davis on a picnic this afternoon. That's what we call it when we prepare our food and eat it outside somewhere."

"Well, thank you, Dr. Simms. You and Mrs. Simms are so thoughtful, and I know that Mr. Davis and I would really appreciate doing that. Would it be too much of a problem if we went out tomorrow afternoon instead?"

"I don't think so," answered Ken with a puzzled look on his face. "Why do you ask?"

"Remember the time you and Mrs. Simms gave me hot dogs to eat?"

"Yes, I remember," responded Ken, looking even more puzzled. "But what has that to do with going on our picnic?"

"Well, at the time we ate the hot dogs, I told you and Mrs. Simms that I wanted to treat you to my favorite food—manioc dipped in caterpillar sauce." Ken and Paul looked at each other—feeling a bit ill.

"You told me at that time it would be nice if we waited for Mr. Davis to return so he could enjoy the treat, too. Well, I've waited, and he has finally arrived. I brought my cook, Samuel, with me and tonight we are going to sit down to a real Banda feast. We're going to have manioc dipped in caterpillar sauce."

Marge Simms entered the room. She held her hand to her nose and was about to speak when Chief Paul called to her.

"Good morning, Mrs. Simms. You're just in time to hear the good news. Tonight Samuel is going to cook some manioc and heat up my caterpillar sauce. I've been saving the sauce for months now. You see, the food calls for a special kind of caterpillar, and they only come out a certain time of the year. That's why I've had to save them."

"Where . . . where . . . is the sauce?" Marge asked hesitantly.

"Oh, it's in my room," said the African, laughing. "I didn't want anything to happen to it so I kept it beside my bed. I can hardly wait until tonight."

"Right," said Ken, looking at Marge. "Neither can we."

8
Disturbing News

"Good-bye, Chief Paul," called Marge from the cab of the pickup truck. "Thanks again for your special treat."

Ken and Paul shook hands with the village chief and headed back toward the truck. The African chief had been with them for the past four days and thought it best to get back to his village.

"Good-bye, my friends," responded the tall leader. "I enjoyed being with you. Since you enjoyed my special treat so much, I'll do it again for you the next time I come."

The two men climbed into the cab. Ken started the motor and the truck moved slowly onto the main road and headed back to Yanga Two. As soon as they were out of sight, Ken looked at his wife.

"Did I hear Chief Paul right? Did he say he would treat us again with his special dish?"

"You heard correctly, honey," answered Marge, laughing. "I guess we made too much of a fuss over that manioc and caterpillar sauce."

"I don't even want to think of it," said Paul. "It was all I could do to eat it. I thought for sure I would be sick from it, but here we are—all well and happy."

Ken laughed out loud. "You two just have weak stomachs, that's all there is to it. Why, I even took seconds."

"That's why Chief Paul is going to do it for us again. You were too convincing, Ken," spoke up Marge.

"All I can say," said Paul, "is that I'm glad my tastes are

different. I suppose, though, if I were born and raised here, I would look upon manioc and caterpillar sauce as a delicacy."

The sun was high in the sky when the trio arrived back at the mission station. Waiting in the driveway beside the house was the mail carrier from the administrator's office in town. The government official always saw to it that the mail for the missionaries was taken out to them, even though the station was located four miles outside town.

Ken Simms took the bag of mail from the messenger. The arrival of the mail was always an exciting time for the American missionaries. The medical doctor opened the bag and carefully emptied its contents onto a nearby table.

"There's one from the home office, honey," said Marge, picking up the large airmail envelope from the States.

"And here's one from Martin and Marie," added Ken. "I wonder how things are shaping up for school. I'm sure they are really excited."

"I wonder what news this one brings," spoke Marge, holding up one from Ann Steele. "We sure are going to have some fun reading this batch of mail."

Ten minutes later the three missionaries sat in the living room reading their mail. Since the news from some of the letters involved the Simmses as well as Paul Davis, Ken read them out loud. The first letter Ken read was from the home office foreign secretary.

" 'By now you no doubt have heard from Mrs. Ann Steele. She visited with us the other day and all were greatly impressed. She is an exceptionally mature woman who wants the Lord's will for her life. Your letter welcoming her to come arrived two days ago, and we immediately called her to let her know. Her papers are satisfactory to us, so we will present them at our next Candidate Committee meeting which will be tomorrow.' "

The next letter to be read was from Ann Steele. The two men listened as Marge read. " 'It seems as though I already know all of you. I've been praying for each of you by name and I'm anxious to meet you. The mission called today and read me your letter of welcome. This is another of the many answers to prayer. Last week my brother, who is in the Air Force, told me he wanted to help with my passage. You can imagine my surprise when he said he wanted to give me one thousand dollars. I wanted to share this good news with you so you can rejoice with me.' "

"Praise the Lord," said Paul. "It looks as if the Lord is putting his approval on Ann's trip to Africa this summer."

"Yes, it does," agreed Ken, "and we need to plan how best to use her talents. I'm sure she will want to be kept busy."

The next letter to be shared by the three friends was from Martin and Marie. The letter was written by Marie.

" 'For the past three weeks, Martin has been suffering from soreness and pain in his right side. He finally went to see a doctor, who ran a number of tests. The doctor wants Martin to go into a hospital that specializes in tropical diseases. We don't know what this all means, but we are trusting the Lord for His will to be done. Martin's eyes are jaundiced and he has lost four kilos. He doesn't seem to have any appetite.' "

"That doesn't sound good," said Marge. "What do you think it could be, Ken?"

"It could be a number of things," responded the doctor. "Jaundice and pain in the liver could be serious. I'm sure Marie will keep us informed."

After reading their mail, the three friends decided to walk over to the workmen's village located alongside the mission station. Before they were half-way there, the children of the village came running to meet them.

"Hello, Dr. Simms," called the one in the lead. "Can we walk with you to the village?"

"You sure can, Ngonde," answered the doctor. "Here, give me your hand." The other children giggled and crowded around the three missionaries. In a few minutes the Americans stood in the middle of the village. Pastor Kondo heard their voices and came out of his house to greet them.

"Good afternoon, my friends," said the smiling pastor. "And what brings you to our humble village?"

"Your friendship," grinned Paul, knowing how Pastor Kondo liked to play on words. The pastor accompanied the missionaries as they made their way around the village.

"What do you hear from Martin and Marie?" asked an elderly man. "I've been burdened to pray for them lately."

"We just received a letter today," responded Ken. "Martin is not well. He is jaundiced and suffering from pain in his right side."

The old man clicked his tongue while slowly nodding his head. "He probably has the water disease, Dr. Simms. Most of our people have it, but it is harder on some than others. It sounds like it."

"What's the water disease, Ken?" whispered Marge.

"It's schistosomiasis," said Ken softly. "Some people can have it for years while others will die in a short time."

"I can see why they would call it the water disease," added Marge. "It sure can fill people up with liquid."

Ken turned to his wife. "There's no doubt that Martin picked up the bug here. If it is an advanced case, it could be very bad for him."

Paul was standing near Kondo and began a conversation with him. "I would like to make a two-week trip in the area north of us. Would you give me some suggestions as to who could go with me?"

The African pastor put his hand under his chin. "How about me, Mr. Davis? I would love to go with you. I'm sure Dr. Simms would be glad to preach here for me, wouldn't you, Dr. Simms?"

"You . . . you know I would, Kondo," the doctor answered happily.

Before Kondo left his missionary friends to return to his house, he and Paul Davis decided upon the date of their trip into the bush. The next four weeks would be a trying time for Paul Davis.

9

Snake!

"We're almost there, Mr. Davis," said Kondo. "As I told you, I have been to this village only once before and that was when I was a boy. My father took me on a hunting trip with him and we stayed here overnight. I'm sure no one will recognize me, but I know there are those who will remember my father."

Several children who were out rat hunting spotted the visitors first. Not accustomed to seeing strangers, the children made a dash for the village.

"We'll have a welcoming party now," said Kondo, laughing.

Within minutes the village was sighted and, as the pastor had predicted, the greater part of the village turned out to investigate the visitors. The village chief was first to welcome the group.

"Welcome to our village. I'm Chief Ndeke."

"Thank you, Chief," responded Pastor Kondo, reaching out to shake the leader's hand. "I'm Pastor Kondo and this is Mr. Davis. We have come to give you and your people good news from God."

"I think I have heard of that good news but I am sure many of my people have not heard it. You are speaking about Jesus, aren't you?"

"That's correct, Chief Ndeke. We would like to stay here until tomorrow morning. We can meet with your people this afternoon and again tonight if you wish."

"I would like that," responded the chief. "And I want you all to be my guests at a meal tonight."

"We accept with happy hearts," said Kondo. Paul's thoughts

went back to the last meal he had had with an African chief. His stomach felt a bit strange.

The chief called several women of the village and instructed them to get the village guesthouse ready for the white man and Pastor Kondo. The other men would be divided among the village households. The rundown guesthouse was located apart from the rest of the village. Since it was only used once or twice a year, the goats found it to be a good shelter.

In an hour, the women had swept it and piled some firewood in front of the grass-roofed mud hut. They also left a large clay pot of water for the men to use for washing.

"This is great," spoke Paul as he and Kondo entered the hut. One of the men traveling with them brought in two folding cots and a duffle bag containing sheets, blankets and mosquito nets. By early afternoon, Paul and Kondo had their temporary house in order. The chief had sent them two folding chairs and a small table that the village carpenter had made.

The meeting that afternoon was attended by everyone present in the village. Many of the villagers had gone to their gardens early in the morning and didn't know about the visitors.

"We will speak to them tonight," Kondo told Paul later. "The chief tells me that this is the first time any of God's people have visited his village. He wants us to stay for several days."

"Well, we're not bound to any schedule, Kondo," replied Paul. "Maybe we should spend more time here in this village."

"Thank the Lord for the seven people who professed Christ as Savior this afternoon. These villagers sure seem hungry for God's Word," added Kondo.

"Snake! Snake!" came the cry from outside the guest hut. Kondo and Paul raced outside to find one of the men of the village poking at a large green snake in the roof of the hut. The eight-foot slender reptile moved with lightning speed, finding a hole in the grass and dropping down inside the hut.

"It's a mamba," said Paul, backing away from the door.

"They are bad," added Kondo. "They attack people without even being provoked. My cousin died from a mamba bite." The villagers began gathering around, many of them with spears and machetes.

"We must kill it," shouted one of the men, "or it may get one of us." Cautiously, several of the men moved toward the open door. One of them pushed his spear into the hut. Nothing happened.

"It's going to wait for one of us to go in," said another man, "and then attack."

One of the goats which had been chased from the hut earlier decided to return. It ran past the men at the entrance and dashed into the hut. Within seconds it cried out, signaling to those outside that the mamba had found a victim. The poor creature made it back to the door and dropped in the entryway. One of the men grabbed it by the leg and pulled it out. It died moments later.

"That's what it is waiting for—one of us to try to go in," said Kondo. Before another word could be said the angry snake came slithering out the door, its head raised three feet off the ground.

"It's attacking!" called Chief Ndeke. The next second, a spear found its mark. One of the men threw a long narrow fishing spear, pinning the mamba to the ground. The wounded, angry reptile whipped its head around, ready to bite anything within range. In a flash, another man lashed out with his machete, taking off the head of the deadly killer.

"Thank You, Lord," whispered Paul to Kondo. "One bite from that creature and it's farewell to life here on earth."

That evening the village was still buzzing with excitement about the mamba. One of the older men of the village took the dead snake and ate it.

"That's so it cannot regain its life and come back again," Kondo explained to Paul.

"But how could it? It was dead. Its head was cut off," Paul questioned.

"I know that and you know that," said the pastor, "but my people still believe it could happen unless someone eats it. You see, Mr. Davis, the Banda people believe that that snake has great powers. That's why the big ones can raise their heads as high as a man's head and still crawl. Its the most feared snake in this country."

Chief Ndeke put on a real feast for the men. Paul was relieved to see that there was no caterpillar sauce. The main part of the meal consisted of manioc with goat meat and chicken. To top off the meal, the chief gave each of the men some wild fruit and strong, black coffee served in tall glasses.

"These glasses are a gift to me from my brother. He bought them in the capital three years ago." Paul knew that the village leader prized the glasses highly and probably only used them for special occasions. The coffee was so strong that Paul could barely drink it. Then, too, it was thick with sugar. Kondo could see that Paul was having difficulty in drinking his coffee.

"My friend, Mr. Davis, would like to put some of this filtered drinking water in his coffee, Chief. He is not used to drinking our strong coffee."

The African chief laughed. "I understand, Pastor. Our ways here in this country are much different from those of your white friend's people."

In a few minutes Kondo was back with a small jar of drinking water for Paul to dilute his coffee. "Thank you, Kondo, for helping me. I want so much to drink coffee with you all, but it was really too strong for me."

Later that night, Kondo and Paul had another service. The Christian men shared their testimonies of how God had saved them, and at the close of the service, eleven of the villagers made public decisions to receive Christ as Savior.

"What a wonderful day," spoke Kondo from inside his mosquito net in the guest hut. "Praise the Lord for the many who were saved."

"Amen," responded Paul. "Even the snake episode brought the people closer to us."

Paul lay awake long after he blew out the kerosene lamp. The thought of the mamba being in that very same hut made him feel uncomfortable. On the other side of the room, Kondo was sound asleep. Every so often he would give out with a snore.

The longer Paul lay there in the pitch darkness, the more uneasy he became. Feeling almost compelled to do so, he reached under his pillow and pulled out his flashlight. He pointed it across the room and turned it on. A chill ran through his body as he gasped. There, stretched out some eight feet under Kondo's camp cot, was an African green mamba. Paul remembered an article he had recently read about mamba snakes. They often travel in pairs.

10

Not
My
Will

Martin Blanc sat in silence as he listened to the doctor give the results of his laboratory tests. The look on his face reflected his concern over the rapid deterioration he had experienced the past six weeks. His jaundiced eyes contrasted sharply with the dark circles around them.

"Our reports show that you have schistosomiasis, Martin. It is possible that the disease has done a considerable amount of damage to your vital organs." The physician wanted to reveal the seriousness of the case and at the same time be careful not to cause his patient undue alarm.

"Please be honest with me, Dr. Grandier. I know what the disease is and what it can do. I've seen it attack the bodies of many of my people in Africa. Besides, I'm ready to die if that is what the Lord wants. I'm not afraid for I know I will go to Heaven to be with my Lord."

The French doctor was surprised to hear Martin speak that way. He looked at Marie, who managed a smile.

"We will start treatment on you immediately, Martin," said Dr. Grandier. "There is a new medicine which has been developed in England. It has had tremendous results. That's all I can tell you at this time."

The next week brought a continued deterioration in Martin's body. The French-African sensed that he was not going to get well. He made that known to Marie one day when she visited him in the hospital.

"I don't believe I'll leave this hospital alive, Marie." As he spoke, it was all the young wife could do to keep back the tears. It was hard on her to watch her beloved husband weaken increasingly. "I have seen enough of this disease in Africa to know what I have and just about what to expect. In fact, my legs are beginning to swell even now. Soon my body will no doubt fill with water."

"But God is able to heal you, Martin," spoke Marie, her words seemingly detached from her.

"I know He can if it's His will. For some reason, however, I don't believe the Lord is going to raise me up." Martin hesitated before continuing. Even the talking tired him out. "God has called you to serve Him, Marie. There is a great need for workers among my tribe. Even though I may not go, you can; and I pray that you will."

Again there was silence as Martin rested. "Dr. deCharles was in to see me today. I told him what I am telling you. I'm sure I will be in Heaven by the time Bible school starts this fall."

"Martin, please!" cried Marie, reaching out to take her husband's hand.

"Don't feel badly, honey. God loves us and He doesn't allow anything to come into our lives that is not for our good and His glory."

"I'm sorry, Martin," responded the young wife. Martin saw the tear trickle from Marie's eye. He squeezed her hand.

"It's only natural for you to feel the way you do, Marie. We've had a wonderful life together since we became Christians. From the human standpoint, I want to serve the Lord with you, but I know we both want God's will for our lives. Isn't that right, honey?"

The young wife nodded her head in agreement, although she was unable to speak. She knew it was only a matter of time until she would be the widow of Martin Blanc.

Late that night Marie wrote letters to their missionary friends. It was impossible for her to keep back the tears as she told of Martin's illness.

"I have just arrived home from the hospital. It has been a week since the doctor gave us the report that Martin has schistosomiasis. In that short time I have seen him fail rapidly. He has lost a lot of weight, is jaundiced and is now beginning to swell with water. I believe my husband will soon be Home with the Lord. He has encouraged me to go to Bible school this fall. I must be honest and say that it will be very difficult to do this without him. All the plans we have made involve us both.

"Dan and Alice are a wonderful help and encouragement to us. Just today, Dan came to the hospital and had prayer with us. How I thank the Lord for these dear friends. With Martin failing so quickly, I'm sure now that it won't be long. The doctor told me that this particular strain of schistosomiasis is the worst kind and that it will gain momentum. Please continue to pray for us. We have both committed ourselves to His holy will."

The next morning Marie awoke with inner peace that only the Lord could give. She called the hospital to get the latest report on Martin's condition.

"He's resting now, Mrs. Blanc. He did have some difficulty last night with pain. We will call you if you are needed."

After breakfast Marie sat down to read her Bible. As she read, her eyes fastened on Psalm 27:14: "Wait on the LORD: be of good courage, and he shall strengthen thine heart: wait, I say, on the LORD." The young wife placed her finger on the verse.

"Father, thank You for Your precious Word. Thank You for the comfort of it. Help me to be brave. I know this is Your will and, Lord, that's what Martin and I want above anything else."

At the hospital Martin opened his eyes and looked around the room. Dan Fine sat nearby.

"Hello, Dan. It's good to see you."

The American smiled as he spoke. "It's about time you acknowledged my presence. Why, I've been here for thirty minutes waiting for you to wake up."

"You are something else, Dan," responded Martin with a crooked smile. "You sure know how to make a fellow feel good."

"I told Alice that I wanted to come over to the hospital and test your patience," continued Dan, trying to look serious. "I guess I'm not very successful; but, then, who cares anyway?"

The two talked for about thirty minutes and then had prayer together. Tears came to Dan's eyes as he listened to his French-African friend talk to the Lord.

"Dear Lord, I thank You for these dear friends You have

brought into our lives. I know I won't be around much longer to enjoy their fellowship but, Father, I'm eagerly looking forward to that fellowship with You. Lord, I pray again for Marie. She is such a good wife. I'm glad she knows and loves You. Father, help her through these difficult days. Please give her peace."

Martin hesitated a moment before he continued. "Now, Father, You know that it is only natural for me to want to get well and enjoy life here with Marie. But if that isn't Your will, then I'm ready to come Home to be with You. Whatever You want for me, Lord, is what I want, too. Not my will, but Yours."

Three days later, Martin slipped quietly into a coma. Marie knew that it would not be long before her beloved husband would be Home with the Lord. Knowing his condition, she prayed it would be soon—very soon.

11
Superstition

Unaware of the deadly mamba snake just eighteen inches below him, Pastor Kondo lay sound asleep. Paul held the flashlight steadily on the eight-foot potential killer. His heart beat hard within him. He knew the devestation in the bite of the reptile.

Kondo stirred and turned on his side, his arm pressing against the mosquito net. The snake moved forward about two feet and lifted its head. Paul knew that the mamba would strike at the slightest movement from Kondo. Its fangs could easily penetrate the net or perhaps even the cot canvas. He wondered what he should do next. The batteries in the flashlight would not last for more than a couple of hours and it was important to know where the snake was at all times. The nervous missionary hesitated to call Kondo for fear that in doing so he might cause the snake to react violently. Mambas were known for their aggressiveness.

"Father," whispered Paul, "show me what I should do. Protect us from the mamba."

Softly Paul began calling Kondo's name. "Kondo! Kondo, wake up! Do you hear me? Wake up!"

The African pastor stirred and opened his eyes. "What's wrong?" he called out. "Paul . . . Paul, is something wrong?" He sat up in his cot, reaching for his flashlight under the pillow.

"Sit still, Kondo. Don't move," whispered Paul. "There's a mamba under your cot."

The African pastor immediately understood the great danger. Moving no more than necessary, he switched on his light. Slowly he moved his head and spotted the mamba beyond the foot of his cot. He could easily see the long line at the side of the snake's jaw giving the appearance that the creature was smiling.

"What are we doing to do, Kondo?" questioned the missionary. "Any move by us could put that snake into a rampage."

The African answered in a low voice. "We must both lie perfectly still. Keep in the middle of your bed as much as possible. We'll turn off our lights and see what happens. I think it's looking for its mate and it may follow its path out the door."

"But that's where its mate was killed," said Paul. "The snake's trail ends there."

"True," answered Kondo, "but at least that will get it out of the hut."

The two men remained silent for several minutes after turning off their lights. Kondo was the first to speak.

"I want you to turn on your light, Mr. Davis. See if the snake has moved."

Without moving, Paul switched on his flashlight. Lying on his side facing Kondo's bed, he could easily see the other half of the hut. "It has moved, Kondo. It is closer to the doorway."

"It definitely is looking for its mate," said Kondo. "I'm sure it knows that something is wrong."

Paul knew that the Africans feared all snakes, including the non-poisonous kind. It was the general belief among the Africans, as well, that the mamba was not only the most dangerous because of its bad disposition and aggressiveness, but also the most intelligent in the snake family.

The men once again lay silently in the dark hut. The thought of the snake being in the hut with them sent a cold chill rippling through Paul's body. Any mistake on their part could mean death. There was no room for a mistake and both men knew that. Ten minutes passed before Kondo spoke again.

"Turn your light on, Mr. Davis. See if you can locate the mamba."

Paul raised himself up and looked around the hut. The snake was gone!

"It's gone, Kondo! I don't see it anywhere."

"It's either outside or it has crawled up the wall into the grass roof," spoke the pastor. "I know one thing for sure, that snake is not going to leave here right away. Mambas have a mind of their own and our older men say the snake will trick you so it can eventually bite and kill you."

Paul realized that even though Kondo was a Christian, there were still many tribal beliefs he held to and his remarks about mambas were no doubt some of them. Another ten minutes went by and the men then decided to get out of their cots and take a look around the hut. They each had their clothing and shoes on the foot of their cots so they dressed inside the mosquite nets. Now and then they flashed their lights around the room to make sure the mamba was not on the floor. Carefully they eased out from under the nets, placing their feet on the hard clay floor.

"I don't see it," said Kondo, scanning the grass roof. "Of course, it could be anywhere in there. They can hide well."

The two friends stood for several minutes. They could not be too careful at a time like this. Slowly they made their way to the open door, stooping to get through the low opening. Paul felt uncomfortable having his head so close to the roof. In seconds, both men were outside.

"Thank the Lord," breathed Paul.

"That was a close one, Mr. Davis. I didn't want to say too much in there, but I really didn't think the mamba would leave that fast. In fact, we could have had a very difficult time getting out of the hut."

Within a short time, several of the villagers had joined the two visitors who were busy looking for the snake.

"You men have brought evil into our village," said one of the men standing nearby. "I don't ever remember two mambas being in any of our houses in one day. That has happened today and the spirits are not happy with us."

Paul was surprised to hear the man speak out as he did. Everyone up to that point had been extremely friendly to the visitors.

"What does this mean, Kondo?" Paul asked in a whisper.

"I really don't know, Mr. Davis. We may have to leave in the morning. There are two kinds of snakes that cause my people to fear reprisals when something happens as it did tonight."

"Which ones are they?" asked Paul.

"The mamba and the red cobra."

"Hello, Mr. Davis. Hello, Pastor Kondo." The two men turned to see the village chief appear out of the darkness. He had several men with him. "I heard that another mamba came into my village tonight and it entered your hut."

"Yes, it did, Chief," answered Kondo. "I'm sure it was looking for its mate."

"You are probably right, Pastor, but you know how our people feel about more than one mamba in the same place. The spirits are angry. You men must go as soon as it gets light."

"But, Chief," said Kondo, careful not to raise his voice, "we are men of the only true God. We came all this way through the jungle to give you God's Word and to tell you about Jesus."

"I know," responded the chief, "but I have an entire village to protect. I must think of all of my people at a time like this."

After the villagers left, Paul, Kondo and the men traveling with them sat around a fire. Each household had politely but firmly asked the men to leave their houses. "I've never seen anything like this," said Kondo softly. "I know my people are superstitious, but I never thought they would do this to us."

As soon as it was light enough to travel, the men packed their belongings and left. None of the people came to say good-bye.

"But what about those new believers, Kondo?" Paul asked once they were inside the forest. "Will we be able to contact them again? Is our ministry finished here?"

"I recall another time you were chased from a village, Mr. Davis. It looked bad then, too; but God, in His wonderful way of doing things, not only took you back into that village but saved the chief who commanded you to leave."

"Kondo," said Paul, smiling, "you are so right. This is the Lord's work and not ours. He can open this village for us again. We will pray to that end."

The two friends shook hands. They understood each other's burden for the village they had just left. Somehow, sometime, Paul felt that he would have the joy of meeting those Christians again in their village. He did not know, however, that he would be accompanied by someone very special to him.

12

On Target—
Djabalo

The last bag of cement was lifted gently from the truck and carried to the temporary storehouse at the edge of Yanga One. "That makes forty bags now, Chief Paul," said Ken, peering into the darkened hut. "We'll be able to begin work on the permanent dispensary soon. We should have at least sixty bags of cement on hand before we begin the foundation and pour the floor."

"Those little termites are almost impossible to stop, Dr. Simms," responded the Christian chief. "Why, if they make up their minds to destroy a building, they can riddle it in a few days' time."

"You're so right, Chief Paul. That's why I want to put a lot of cement into the building. You see, there will be lots of valuable medicines and equipment to protect from the ants."

Chief Paul clicked his tongue as he slowly nodded his head. "Before the white men came, we never knew anything about cement. It sure is strange how that powder, when mixed with sand and water, can get so hard."

"Here in your land, Chief, it usually takes longer to build a strong building than it does in my country. There, a machine usually mixes the cement. Here, we do it by hand," explained Ken.

"We may have to do it by hand, Dr. Simms," answered Chief Paul, smiling, "but you must admit, we have lots of hands to use."

"Here come Pastor Kondo and Mr. Davis!" someone shouted from one end of the village. In the distance came the group of weary travelers, walking slowly around a bend in the road. The people of the village gathered to greet the little party of men. Some of the children ran to meet them. Chief Paul waved and called to them.

"Welcome back. Come, tell us of your trip."

The village chief turned to some of the women and told them to bring water so the men could wash. He also gave orders to prepare some chicken and a goat for the evening meal. Along with several basins of washing water, the women brought two large clay bowls of drinking water. The evaporation of the water through the bowls caused the liquid to be cooler than usual. The men drank long from the clay vessels.

That night, Kondo related to the people of Yanga One what had taken place at the village of Djabalo.

"Well, that name suits the village just right," spoke up one of the men. The people laughed at the remark.

"I wonder why they named the village 'Satan,'" murmured Ken, sitting beside Marge.

"I wonder, too," responded Marge. "There must be a lot of Satan worship going on there."

"I'm sure there is," said Ken. "I don't think, however, that this is the end of our dealings with that village. I can almost read Chief Paul's mind right now."

The longer Pastor Kondo spoke, the quieter and more serious the villagers became. When the pastor had finished, Chief Paul stood up to address his people.

"We all know that it isn't the Lord's will for those people to be in such bondage." The village leader spoke slowly, carefully choosing his words. "I came through that village about ten years ago. It is a village to fear if you don't know Jesus as your Savior."

Several of the people clicked their tongues, indicating their agreement with their chief.

"I'm going to make a visit to Djabalo in a few days and I want all of you Christians to pray for me as I go. Satan doesn't want me to go there, but I'm going anyway, and I plan to take Pastor Kondo and Mr. Davis with me."

The village erupted into applause. Several of the men stepped forward to shake the leader's hand.

"Well, it looks like you're going on a trip, Paul," whispered Ken with a grin. "You didn't tell me about your plans."

Paul raised his eyebrows as he met his co-worker's glance. "You're just jealous because the chief is not taking you along." The two friends smiled and then turned their attention to Chief Paul.

"God has a great work to do in this country and I have dedicated myself to Him to help in that work."

"I have, too, Chief," called one of the men as he stood to his feet.

"So have I," added another.

"We know what it is like to worship Satan," Chief Paul continued. "Most of us were saturated with witchcraft. We have seen the power of the devil."

The Simmses and Paul arrived home late. Before they left Yanga One, Paul and Pastor Kondo arranged to come back in three days to make the trip to Djabalo with Chief Paul.

The night guard at the mission station sat beside a small fire out in front of his hut in the backyard. Beside him was the mail bag which the administrator at the post had sent out that afternoon.

"Well, there's our week's mail," said Marge, pointing to the canvas bag. "I wonder how Martin is doing."

Ken met the guard halfway to the house and gladly relieved him of the sack of mail. Inside the house he pushed the starter button for the gasoline-driven power plant. In seconds the room was flooded with light. Marge pulled the tablecloth off and folded it neatly.

"Empty the mail onto the table, Ken. It's easier to sort that way," spoke the pretty wife.

As the pieces of mail were spread out on the table, Marge spotted the French stamps immediately. "There's one from Martin and Marie," she said excitedly.

"It only has Marie's name on it," Paul added, pointing to the return address. "I wonder why she did that."

The rest of the mail remained untouched as the three friends shared the news in the letter from France.

" 'I sent you a telegram as soon as Martin died, but this is the first opportunity I have had to write to you. The Lord called him Home on June 2.' "

Marge's eyes filled with tears. "Martin's dead," she whispered, slowly shaking her head. "We must let Marie know as soon as possible that we didn't receive her telegram."

Ken continued reading. " 'He had an acute case of schistosomiasis which caused him to fail rapidly. He went into a coma and never regained consciousness.' "

"And to think," said Ken, looking up from the letter, "that perhaps as many as eighty percent of the Africans in this area are infected with this horrible disease."

" 'Dan preached a wonderful message at the funeral service. I was greatly surprised that my parents attended. Other than what I have written to them, it was the only other source from which they have heard the gospel.' "

"Praise the Lord," exclaimed Paul. "I don't know much about Marie's family, but I know she has a great burden for them."

" 'I have saved the most heartening news until last. You all know of Mr. Henry Duval and his efforts to get us to rejoin the Party. We have been praying that God would bring him back into our lives. Well, he happened to be visiting my parents when they received my telephone call of Martin's death. He attended the funeral with them and I had the wonderful opportunity to talk with him about the Lord. Just before he left with my parents, he accepted Christ as his Savior. Please pray for him as his life is now in danger because of his being a Christian. Pray for Mrs. Duval, too, that she will come to know Christ as her Savior.' "

"Thank the Lord," said Paul. "What a great answer to prayer."

" 'Even though the Lord has called Martin to Heaven, I intend to go to Bible college. Dr. deCharles told me I could start this semester or begin in January at mid-term. I'm looking forward to the day when I will be there working with you.' "

"I'm anxious to meet Marie," interrupted Marge. "She sounds like she will really fit into the work here."

"I'm sure she will, honey," agreed Ken.

The three co-workers again turned their attention to the letter which Ken held. " 'Please share this news with Chief Paul. Martin was his adopted brother and I know he will want to hear what has happened. I'm writing a letter to Chief Paul in this same mail and am addressing the envelope in care of the mission station. Your letter contains more details and it is for that reason I'm asking you to share the contents of my letter with the chief.' "

"There's Chief Paul's letter right there," Marge said, pointing to an envelope showing Marie's address. "And here's one from Ann Steele, too. I wonder what news she has for us."

A strange feeling ran through Paul as he saw the delicate handwriting on the envelope. He hoped Ken would choose that letter to read next.

13
The Amazing Chief Paul

"July 30th it is my friends," Ken glanced up from the letter he was reading from Ann Steele.

"I'm sure it will seem good for you to have another woman around, Marge. You must feel outnumbered by us two men."

"Oh, so you think I'm outnumbered, do you? Well, for your information, Ken Simms, I can call on Chief Paul any time for his backing."

The three missionaries laughed together, knowing there was a close tie binding them together. Paul always felt comfortable with them and made it a point now and then to tell them of his feelings.

"That's only two weeks away," spoke Paul, glancing at the calendar on the wall. "I think that while she's here, I'll move to Yanga One. The guesthouse that Chief Paul constructed there is very comfortable and I really wouldn't mind living there for a few months."

"But what happens when we come to visit Yanga One?" said Marge, winking at Ken.

"No problem," responded Paul. "I'll move in with Chief Paul or even move into the dispensary hut." As they kidded about the situation, the missionaries began to see there would be a housing problem with Ann Steele added to their team.

"I'm going to be with Chief Paul in a few days," spoke Paul. "Suppose I ask him if his men can put up a small hut for Ann so she can visit Yanga One. They're so happy to get her help, I'm sure they will do anything they can to make her comfortable."

The next two days went by quickly. Pastor Kondo received a hand-carried letter from Tene that he would rather wait until the following summer to marry Kondo's daughter Ruth. That way, he would be graduated from Bible school and ready to devote himself to building a house—probably at Yanga One. The general feeling among the Christian community was that this was mature thinking on Tene's part and that the decision was a good one.

Ken and Marge took Paul and Kondo to Yanga One and then immediately returned to Yanga Two to get ready for their trip to the capital for Ann Steele. For their hike into the jungles to reach the village Djabalo, Chief Paul chose ten of his best-trained men who were skilled in jungle travel and could cope with nearly any situation they would encounter.

The day they left, the villagers of Yanga One turned out to bid their chief farewell. "We'll be praying for you, Chief Paul," called one of the young men in the crowd. As the group of men moved out of the village on to the main road, those remaining behind broke out into a hymn.

> We have heard the joyful sound:
> Jesus saves! Jesus saves!
> Spread the tidings all around;
> Jesus saves! Jesus saves!

Paul turned to look at the villagers. He thought of the day he had been ordered from the village by the same man who now was leading the evangelistic team to a village closed to the gospel. A smile spread across the missionary's face.

"Thank you, Father, for what You have done here at Yanga One. Thank You for allowing me to be part of this great miracle."

The men traveled until dusk and stopped beside a small stream. There they set up camp for the night. Chief Paul, Pastor Kondo and Paul had folding camp cots, which they quickly put up. They had some army surplus mosquito nets which Paul had brought out with him his first term. For his part of the food supply, Paul had brought several pounds of cube sugar and four dozen cans of sardines. He knew how his African friends liked their coffee sweet and sardines were a treat to anyone at any time.

Chief Paul gave orders to one of the men who doubled as his cook to roast some manioc sticks. The black coffee boiling away soon sent a tempting aroma throughout the camp. The men found some banana trees nearby and cut several leaves to serve as plates for the sardines. It was amusing to Paul to see how each man produced some kind of a drinking utensil for the coffee. Chief Paul had his favorite tall glass which he filled to the top with the strong brew and then proceeded to drop ten cubes of sugar into it.

While they were eating, a woman appeared, on her way to her village from her garden. She had a large stalk of ripe bananas on her head. Chief Paul asked her if she would like to sell them. Upon receiving her positive reply, he promptly purchased the entire stalk.

"Just look at those stars up there, Chief Paul," said Paul as the men sat around the fire. "They look small but they really are many times bigger than the sun, moon and earth on which we live."

"For us, that's hard to understand, Mr. Davis. But because you say it, we believe it," answered the African leader. The chief spread out his arms. "When I see all this around me, I just thank my God that I know Him—the One Who made it all."

"That's right, Chief Paul," spoke Kondo, "and the importance of all these things can't begin to come up to how much value we are to God."

"That's beautiful, Kondo," said Chief Paul. "You have said it just the way I think, but I can't put it in words like that."

Now and then one of the men would stir the fire or put a stick on it, sending the sparks flying high into the air. Some of the men had already drifted off to sleep.

"Before we all get so sleepy that we can't sing, I want Mr. Davis to lead us in some hymns. We'll start with, 'When the Roll Is Called Up Yonder,' Mr. Davis."

Paul knew that the well-known hymn was Chief Paul's favorite. Pitching it low enough so all the men could hit the notes, the American began singing. Immediately he was joined by the men, singing loudly:

> When the roll is called up yonder,
> When the roll is called up yonder,
> When the roll is called up yonder,
> When the roll is called up yonder,
> I'll be there.

Chief Paul wiped the tears from his eyes, cleared his throat and spoke to the men. "I never sing this song but what I think of my brother, Kota. I'll never forget how he accepted Jesus as his Savior just seconds before he died." The leader then extended his hand to Paul. "Thank you, Mr. Davis, for bringing the good news of Jesus to us. Our lives have never been the same since we trusted Him."

The men were on the trail by daybreak. Chief Paul wanted to reach the village of Djabalo before too late in the afternoon. The men sang hymns as they made their way along the narrow jungle path. Every now and then Paul would hear Chief Paul's deep voice hang on to a note longer than the other men. The village leader enjoyed everything about his salvation and loved to hear himself sing praises to God.

"Stop!" shouted one of the men in the lead. Several of the men dove into the underbrush. There, stuck in the center of their path, was an arrow, its shaft still vibrating.

"Chief Ndeke means business," Chief Paul whispered to Paul and Kondo. He spoke loud enough for all of his men to hear him. "You men stay right where you are. I don't want anyone to move. Chief Ndeke has men out there in the jungle and they have orders to shoot us if we approach the village past this point."

The tall leader from Yanga One strode forward past the arrow, walking at a brisk pace. Some fifty feet beyond the arrow he stopped and cupped his hands to his mouth. "You men out there, I want you to listen to me. I am the grandson of Canton Chief Bira. His name is known by all of you. I remain his only descendent and I carry his authority. Now come out and come out quickly."

Paul and Kondo stared at each other. "I didn't know that Chief Paul was Chief Bira's grandson," said the African pastor.

"Who was Chief Bira?" questioned Paul, somewhat amazed at still another strange piece of information concerning Chief Paul.

"He was the most feared chief the Banda tribe ever knew," answered Pastor Kondo. "No one ever opposed him. Our ears have been filled with stories of the great things he did. His power was unparalleled in this whole country."

Within moments, eighteen warriors stood before Chief Paul. There was not a sign of opposition among them.

"Now you will lead me to your chief. He, too, will accept me like you have. I have some good news to share with all of you at Djabalo and I don't intend to return to Yanga One until everyone in the village has heard what I have to say."

Chief Paul motioned for his group to follow him. He then pointed up the path. "All right, men. Let's go. I want to get to your village before the sun falls to the tops of the hills."

Paul and Kondo hurried to catch up with Chief Paul. "I didn't know you were the grandson of Chief Bira," spoke Pastor Kondo. "You come from a famous line of people."

"My grandfather was so wicked I don't like to let people know I'm related to him. However, today I did it because I know these men needed to hear something which would put fear in them. We must pray that Chief Ndeke will receive us now. He could be very angry that we got by his men. I'm sure they have been following us for some distance."

Paul Davis was quite sure the chief of Djabalo would accept them. The battle for the village of Satan was taking a turn for the good, and he was anxious to see what kind of reception they would have from those who had chased them away a short time before.

14
Miracle at 'Good News'

The closer the group got to the village of Djabalo, the more tense the men became. Chief Paul seemed to show no excitement as he led the group, followed by Chief Ndeke's men and then by his own. Pastor Kondo and Paul dropped back into their own group at the suggestion of the African leader.

Several village dogs signaled the arrival of the visitors and within minutes every hut was emptied. As the men came around the last turn in the path, there standing in front of his people was Chief Ndeke.

"I heard you were coming, Ngonjo, but I'm surprised to see you. How did you get by my guards?"

Chief Paul continued walking until he stood an arm's length from his fellow-chief. "It was no problem, Ndeke," responded the respected leader of Yanga One. "You may have forgotten that I'm the grandson of Canton Chief Bira. That makes me the inheritor of his authority."

Chief Ndeke stood in silence as he listened to the visiting chief. Even though the canton chief had died many years before, tribal custom demanded that respect be given former leaders. The villagers stood quietly as the two men spoke.

"I hear you, Ngonjo," responded Chief Ndeke. "What brings you and these men to my village? Just this past week the spirits warned us to make some of these same men leave our village. Don't they have any respect for our gods?"

"No, they don't, Ndeke. And I don't either. You see, we are not bound by those fears anymore. Jesus has set us free. He has given us life and hope beyond physical death."

"That's what they told us, too. And then the mambas came. You know what that means, Ngonjo. You know all our beliefs."

"Yes, I know what it means when two mambas appear in one place, but that doesn't frighten me anymore. My God is much more powerful than those things, Ndeke."

Chief Paul hesitated and then continued. "And, besides, I'm not 'Ngonjo' anymore. When Jesus came into my life and saved me, He changed me completely. At that time, I took a new name. I'm Paul now, Ndeke. The Paul in God's Book was a strong worker for God. I want to be like him. We all know that Ngonjo is 'bitter' and 'mean.' That isn't me anymore, Ndeke. I'm different."

Chief Paul's words seemed to stun the people of Djabalo. When he had finished speaking, he put out his hand to Chief Ndeke. "I'm glad to see you again, Ndeke. It's been many years since you and I worked with the witch doctor and the Yondo camp. Don't worry about anything bad happening to your village because of our presence. I've asked my God to protect you and your people."

"Thank you," said Chief Ndeke, his voice giving away his uncertainty. "You are welcome to my village."

"I don't plan to visit any other villages on this trip, Ndeke," spoke Chief Paul. "I came to be here with you and your people so I'm asking you to give us lodging and food."

Within the hour, Chief Paul had moved in with Chief Ndeke. Pastor Kondo and Paul were directed to the guest hut and the rest of the men scattered around in the village houses. Upon entering the guest hut, a chill ran through Paul's body. How well he remembered the experience that he and Kondo had with the mambas only several days earlier in this same hut.

"I can hardly believe, Kondo, that just a few days ago you and I slept in this hut with a deadly mamba."

"It's even more difficult to believe that we are back in this village so soon after being chased out," added Kondo.

"God sure works in mysterious ways, Kondo. The way He has brought us back here to Djabalo is a miracle. I can hardly wait to see what happens while we're here."

The men had a service that night with Chief Paul giving his personal testimony. He spoke for two hours, giving all the details of such events as when he chased Paul Davis and Dr. Simms from Yanga One, his conversion, his brother Kota's death, Tene's conversion, his mother's influence at Yanga One, Martin Blanc's arrival on the scene and the permission to build a permanent dispensary at Yanga One.

"We hope soon to have the dispensary built and we need a nurse for it. I hear there is a young widow coming out in two weeks so I can't stay any longer than a few days. I must get back and get things ready for her to do her work."

Paul smiled as he listened to Chief Paul's words.

"Now we're going to have a meeting early tomorrow morning. We'll have another one in the afternoon and one tomorrow night before we go to bed. We want everyone to attend every meeting. Isn't that right, Ndeke?"

Chief Paul glanced over at his host. Chief Ndeke clicked his tongue while nodding his head. The leader from Yanga One had an unusual way of winning the confidence of the people. Suddenly Paul Davis felt comfortable about being in Djabalo.

The next afternoon, Chief Paul promised the people of Djabalo there would be a special announcement in the evening service. That night it seemed that a larger group was present to hear the announcement. After the Yanga One men sang a few hymns for the people of Djabalo, Chief Paul stood up to speak.

"My friends, there are two very important things to say to you. Until a short time ago, there was only one, but now there are two. I will announce mine first; then Chief Ndeke wants to speak."

A buzz rippled through the crowd that gathered in the early evening darkness. A faint light in the western sky was the last remains of the day's sun. The sky overhead was dotted with stars. Now and then a dog would bark at something in the nearby forest. The fire in the center of the large circle cast eerie shadows. Chief Paul stepped a bit closer to the fire. His tall stature added to his demand for respect.

"What I have to say I have discussed with your chief as well as with our missionary friend, Mr. Davis. Both are in full agreement." He paused a moment to allow the words to make their impact and then continued. "For as long as you can remember, you have suffered with all kinds of sickness. The only medicine you had was what you made yourselves from roots, bark, leaves and even from certain wild fruits. All of you have offered sacrifices and prayed to gods you do not know."

As the chief spoke, the clicking of tongues could be heard throughout the crowd. "Well I have a proposition to make to you. If you will build a house of God for us to preach in when we come, and a dispensary, we will try to make regular trips to your village to give you God's Word and also to treat your sores and diseases."

Before Chief Paul could say another word, the people began to shout and clap their hands. His words met with full approval of the villagers.

"I don't know who the nurse will be but I know my God will see that there is someone to come." The chief's simple faith was a blessing to behold. If he felt that God was in it, then he believed it would come to pass. The missionaries often marveled at his childlike trust in the Lord. Large problems or small—they all seemed the same to him.

"And now your chief has something very important to say to you." Chief Ndeke stood up and looked around the group. He spoke with a very serious tone in his voice.

"My people, I am not the same man you have known for these many years. Something happened in my hut which has changed my thinking and will affect the way I live from now on."

The people of Djabalo looked at each other, wondering what their leader was saying. They never had heard him speak like this before.

"Since Chief Paul's arrival, he has been talking to me about Jesus, his Savior. Last night we talked until nearly daylight. Early this afternoon we took a walk into the forest where we could be alone. I had many questions but he answered all of them. My people, I have accepted Jesus as my Savior. Now I'm asking you, too, to accept Him into your hearts. God has forgiven me of my wicked sins and He has made me His child. As Chief Paul explained it, he and I are true brothers now because God is our Father.

Chief Ndeke turned to shake Chief Paul's hand. The two leaders stood together to show their unity in what was said. "Now there are two more things I want to say," Ndeke continued. "Listen carefully. Beginning tomorrow, I will appoint a number of you men to start making blocks for the new house of God and the house of medicines. We must cut grass before the fires come so some of you women will be asked to cut roofing grass. I'm appointing my village foreman, Bamara, to oversee the work."

Again the crowd buzzed with excitement but it was a good response. Paul sensed a strong support for the chief.

"The second thing does not involve work, but it does require cooperation from each of you. We will not be known any longer as the village of Djabalo. Satan is the enemy of our souls and I don't want anything to do with him, especially having our village named after him. From now on, my people, we will be known as the village of Tene Ndjoni."

The new name brought forth another reaction from the villagers. Several clapped their hands. Paul nodded his head in agreement with the new name, which meant "Good News."

"You will remember when Mr. Davis and Pastor Kondo visited us several days ago. One of the first things they said was that they had good news to give to us." As Chief Ndeke spoke, Paul could see many of the heads nodding their approval of their chief's words.

"Yesterday, when Chief Paul and his men arrived, one of the first things he said was that he had good news for us. I can't think of a better name for our village than 'Good News.' What do you all think about that name?"

Without exception, the people applauded their leader. Paul was overwhelmed. So many things were happening in such a short time. Miracle after miracle was taking place before his eyes.

Two days later, the party from Yanga One left the village of Good News. Chief Ndeke, along with a number of his people, accompanied the visitors for about an hour. Before they parted, the two groups sang a hymn and Pastor Kondo prayed. Not only were there many warm handshakes, but several of the men who had become close friends blew into each other's ears. Knowing this was a special Banda greeting for family members, Paul realized again the tremendous impact Chief Paul and his group of men had made on the people of Good News. The two groups shouted to each other as long as their voices could be heard. All were invited to visit each other's homes. That night as the Yanga One party camped, Chief Paul asked each of them to give thanks to the Lord for the miracle at Good News.

As he stretched out in his cot under the stars, Paul felt good inside. He wondered if he might have a part in the Lord's work of establishing a church and medical work at Good News.

15

Join the Club

The squeal of the tires of the large DC-8 could be heard across the airport as the missionaries stood on the deck of the terminal. The rubber hitting the pavement sent puffs of smoke into the air.

"She's down," said Dale Banks, peering through a pair of binoculars.

"It won't be long now until we meet Ann Steele," added Ken.

The two couples waited until the big plane taxied to the terminal and began unloading its passengers. Dale trained the glasses on the front door of the airliner.

"I . . . I . . . think that's her in the green dress. She seems to be looking for someone."

The missionaries made their way down the steps to the door through which the passengers would come after going through customs and the police inspections.

"There she is," said Ken, waving to the pretty woman in the green dress.

"She's beautiful," breathed Marge.

"She sure is," said Dale, grinning as he winked at Ken.

"O.K., you fellows," Dorothy Banks laughed. "Any more remarks like that and you both get bread and water for a week."

In ten minutes, Ann Steele walked through the door, meeting her co-workers for the first time. "I am so glad to be here," she said as the introductions were made. "I've looked forward to this for a long time."

The missionaries all talked at once as they questioned the newcomer about news from the States. Finally they made their way to the car. Twenty minutes later, the two couples and Ann arrived at the mission station.

"I never expected to see anything like this in the heart of Africa," remarked Ann as she saw the buildings for the first time.

"I guess we all thought the same thing," said Marge. "I expected to sleep in a grass-roofed, mud hut when I first came. There is a big difference once you leave the capital city. Even though you see modern civilization here in the city, the moment you pass the city limits you will see the way people lived fifty years ago. There has been very little progress as far as homes, furniture and the way of life are concerned."

"I'm so excited," said Ann, her dark brown eyes twinkling as she spoke. "I want to make the next three months as full as possible. I'm here to learn all that I can so please feel free to pass on to me as much information as you wish."

"I'm sure you are tired from your trip," spoke Dorothy. "The time change will affect you for a few days. If you wish to take a nap, please do so. We plan to take you to a French restaurant tonight."

"Wonderful," responded Ann. "I've heard a lot about French cuisine, and just think, I am actually going to eat in a French restaurant. I never did leave the airport in Paris. There were only four hours between my flights."

Ann Steele immediately won the hearts of her new friends. After she retired to her bedroom, the two couples expressed their thanks to the Lord for sending a short-term worker with such sweet qualities.

"She must have been a wonderful wife and mother," said Dorothy. "I've only known her for a couple of hours and already I feel a real love for her."

"The Lord sent her to us," Ken added, "and I'm sure she'll be a good missionary."

"The people will love her," chimed in Dale.

"I'm wondering what Paul will think of her," spoke Marge, knowing of her co-worker's loneliness. "Sometimes he seems really lost without Becky. I know he deeply misses her."

That night the new missionary expressed her thankfulness

over and over for everyone's kindness to her. "I can't believe it's really me here in Africa. And that you dear friends invited me to come with you for a French meal. This is a treat I'll always remember. Thank you so very much."

Two days later the Simmses and Ann started the two-day trip to Yanga Two. As they rode along, Ken and Marge shared with Ann the story of Yanga One. Tears came to her eyes when they told her about the Homegoing of Becky Davis.

"Mr. Davis must be a very dedicated man to return as he did. I'm anxious to see him again—even though I didn't really speak to him the first time I saw him."

Now and then the three would sing together as they rode along the winding dirt road. Ann's singing voice was just as beautiful as her looks and their voices blended well together.

By the time they arrived at the Bible school station, the three travelers were very weary. Their clothing as well as their skin was red from the road dust. Ken drew a laugh from his co-workers when he took off his sunglasses. The only clean place on his face was around his eyes.

"You'll welcome a shower after this trip," Marge said to Ann as they emerged from the cab of the pickup. "Sometimes it seems to take two or three showers to get all the dirt off."

Bill and Kathy Dykes took to Ann immediately. Kathy told the newcomer how much she reminded her of her younger sister. "You both look so much alike, you could pass for sisters. Her husband is a pastor in Michigan."

To top the evening off, Bill and Ken made a big batch of popcorn. "We've been saving this for a special occasion," said Bill, "and I don't know of anything more special than welcoming a new missionary."

"But I'm only a short-termer," said Ann, smiling.

"Maybe the Lord will call you here as a full-timer. Wouldn't that be great?" added Ken.

"That would be marvelous," Kathy joined in.

That night Ann lay in bed thinking of their conversation about full-time missionary service. "Father," she prayed, "I would count it a privilege if You would call me here to work for You permanently." A tear trickled down the side of her face. "I only have one life to live for You, Lord. My only desire is to live that life in Your will." Her lips were still moving in prayer as she drifted off to sleep.

The Simmses and Ann planned to leave early the next morning for Yanga Two. Tene was at the pickup to meet them when they came out of the house. He had an envelope in his hand.

"Dr. Simms, would you please give this to Ruth for me? Give my greetings to the Christians in the workmen's village and tell Pastor and Mrs. Kondo that I send my love."

Bill and Kathy stood beside the truck, which was surrounded by a number of Bible school students. Before Ken started the motor, Tene led in prayer asking the Lord's protection upon the missionaries as they traveled.

"And, Lord," he prayed, "we thank You for Mrs. Steele. It's going to be hard for her out here by herself just like it is for Mr. Davis. So, Father, we pray for both of them as well as for the married couples. We thank You for sending these missionaries to us."

When Tene finished his prayer, a chorus of "amens" could be heard from the students. After they started down the main road, Ken turned to Ann.

"I wish you could have understood Tene's prayer. It would have touched your heart. He prayed for both you and Paul Davis. He mentioned how hard it is for you two to be out here without companions, and he simply asked the Lord to help you."

"That was really wonderful of him," said Ann.

Late in the afternoon the pickup turned down the long driveway at the mission station. To the surprise of Ken and Marge, Paul Davis sat on the front veranda with Pastor Kondo. The two men walked to the driveway to meet the Simmses and Ann as the three weary travelers stepped down from the truck. Ken and Paul shook hands.

"Paul," said Ken, "this is Ann Steele."

Ann reached her hand out to Paul. "How do you do, Mr. Davis. I'm glad to meet you."

"Hello, Ann, I'm happy to see you made it. Welcome to Yanga Two. I hope you will find it to be the wonderful place I told about in your home church."

Ann smiled, showing a dimple on each cheek. "I know I'm

going to love it, Mr. Davis. I'm anxious to get to work."

Ken gave the envelope to Pastor Kondo for his daughter Ruth. Knowing the missionaries were tired from their trip, the African Christians headed back to their village after giving their usual greetings.

"The administrator stopped at Yanga One to see Chief Paul and offered a ride to Kondo and me, so here we are," explained Paul. "Since the medical apartment is empty, I thought I would stay out there until I return to Yanga One. I'm going to need some supplies other than sardines and coffee." Ken and Marge laughed.

"What Paul is saying is that he had to come home to get his food supplies. There's only one small store in the village of Yanga One, and the two things one can always find in the line of food is coffee and sardines." Ken said.

"Sardines!" said Ann, laughing. "You may think I'm crazy, but I love sardine sandwiches."

"Welcome to the club," spoke Paul, reaching out to shake her hand. "That's one of my favorites, too."

As Paul walked out to the medical apartment later that night, he looked up into the star-studded sky. "Dear Father," he prayed, "somehow I feel different tonight. Some of the lonely feeling is gone. Thank You, Father, for sending Ann. Give her a blessed time here among these precious Africans."

As Paul dozed off to sleep, he saw before him a pretty face. There was a smile on it and a dimple on each cheek. At the same time, Ann listened to the African night sounds and a smile spread across her face. "That's funny," she whispered, "a sardine sandwich club—and only two members!"

16

'Hello, Mr. Duval'

The ring of the telephone startled Marie Blanc as she sat writing a letter to Ken and Marge Simms. She picked up the receiver to hear a familiar voice on the other end of the line.

"Marie, this is Henry Duval." The young French widow was surprised but glad to hear his voice.

"Hello, Mr. Duval. It's good to hear from you. How are you?"

"I'm fine, Marie. Thank you for praying for me. I told Mrs. Duval of my conversion to Christ, and to my surprise she sat and listened to all that I had to say. Last night we attended a small Protestant church. The pastor, who knows of your missionary friends, spoke about the Bible and Jesus just as you do."

Marie was so excited she hardly knew what to say. "I'm so glad to hear this wonderful news. I have been praying that the Lord would help you share your testimony with Mrs. Duval, and that her heart would be open to what you had to say. God has answered my prayers."

"He surely has," said Mr. Duval. "I know now what you mean when you speak about a personal and powerful God. I have been a different man since Christ saved me." Changing the topic of conversation, Mr. Duval continued. "One of the reasons I'm calling, Marie, is concerning your Bible college training. If I heard you correctly when we spoke at the funeral service, you mentioned that you still planned to go to school. Is that correct?"

"Yes, it is," answered Marie. "The Lord willing, I will be there when it starts in two weeks."

"Well, that's what I thought," answered the former Communist. "I'm calling to tell you that Mrs. Duval and I want to pay your first year's tuition and your room and board." Marie was speechless.

"Are you still there, Marie?"

"Yes, Mr. Duval, I'm still here and I don't know how to thank you and Mrs. Duval for your offer to pay this large amount."

"It's because we really want to do this, my dear. When I think of the great amount of money I have spent personally to spread the Communist propaganda, it grieves me terribly. I'm determined to do all that I can the rest of my life to share the truths about God and His Son, Jesus Christ."

"How can I ever thank you," said Marie, crying softly.

"You don't have to thank us, Marie. The fact that you are preparing to do a work for God is all the thanks that we want. If it is all right with you, however, Mrs. Duval and I would like to visit the college. I think it would be a wonderful experience for her to see young adults like you who love God and are dedicated to His cause, instead of young people we know who are dedicated to the cause of atheistic communism."

That night Marie rewrote her letter to Ken and Marge Simms. Her heart was overflowing with praise to God as she shared with them the conversation she had that day with Henry Duval.

"When Martin died, I felt at times as if the world had caved in on me. All my future plans were combined with his. To be honest with you, I had no thought of the future without Martin. Satan tempted me greatly to think that God had forgotten me or even made a mistake. How thankful I am that we serve a God Who is all-wise and perfect in all that He does. I accept Martin's Homegoing as the will of God for Martin and me. When Mr. Duval called today to tell me that he and Mrs. Duval wanted to pay my full expenses this first year at Bible college, I realized anew that God is in control and that He will direct my paths and supply all my needs. I am eagerly looking forward to going to Bible college.

"Please pray for Mrs. Duval. She listened to Mr. Duval without any opposition as he told her of his conversion and his desire to live for Christ. This is an answer to prayer and I'm confident that someday she, too, will come to know Christ as her Savior.

"I'm so glad to hear that Ann Steele fits in so well and is doing such a great job there at Yanga Two and Yanga One. Being a nurse, I must confess that I get excited as I think of the many opportunities there are to serve the Lord in the field of medicine there in Africa. Four years of college plus perhaps a year or more of securing my funds from the churches seems a long time, especially when I am already excited about coming. I believe, however, that Bible college is my next step, and as far as I'm concerned that is the place of the Lord's will for me."

Finishing her letter, Marie put down her pen and slipped to her knees. "Thank You, Father, for saving me and bringing into my life these wonderful missionary friends. Thank You, too, for saving Mr. Duval. Dear Lord, I ask You to save Mrs. Duval. She needs so desperately to know You. Put just the right words in Mr. Duval's mouth as he talks to her about You. And, Lord, thank You, too, for supplying all my financial needs for my first year of Bible college. You have shown me that that is where You want me."

After she finished praying, Marie remained on her knees. In the quietness of her apartment, she thought back to her years of contact with the Communist Party. A chill ran through her when she realized that if it were not for the grace of God, she would be a Communist agent dedicated to the task of spreading the satanic poison of atheism.

The next two weeks passed quickly for Marie as she packed her personal belongings and prepared to leave her furnished apartment for Bible college. The excitement of Bible school continued to build up within her. Dr. deCharles called to see if there was anything he could do for her. Dan and Alice Fine invited her to stay with them her last few nights in Paris. It was a temptation for Marie to wish that Martin could experience these eventful days with her, but she knew that he was far better off with the Lord.

The Fines offered to take Marie to school and she gladly accepted their invitation. She appreciated their help in getting her settled upon arrival.

The thought of formal Bible training was a bit frightening to Marie as she glanced around the classroom and saw that all the students were younger than she. The second day in class she shared her anxiety with Dr. deCharles.

"Dr. deCharles, I'm rather scared. Most of the students here have come from Christian families where they have heard the Bible for many years. I'm a fairly new Christian and I'm not sure I can keep up with them."

The kind veteran professor looked at Marie. A smile slowly spread across his face. "You will do all right, Marie, You have nothing to worry about. God has given you a good sharp mind. I would say that even your disciplined training in communism will benefit you greatly in your studies here in Bible college. The Lord sent you here, Marie, and I can assure you that there are many wonderful blessings in store for you as you train for the ministry that God has for you."

The words of Dr. deCharles brought a gentle soothing to Marie's fears. Even the kindly professor could not see that one of those blessings would be just twelve months away.

17

A Burden Kindled

Ann Steele adapted well to the African climate. The road between Yanga One and Yanga Two was well traveled as Ken and Paul hauled supplies from the permanent dispensary building. Chief Paul was on the job every day, making sure that the work progressed as quickly as possible. The villagers of Yanga One accepted Ann as their own family. To make her comfortable, Chief Paul had his men construct a building with three rooms. He explained to Ken and Paul that he didn't want the new lady living in a one-room round hut. He wanted her to feel at home, and the best way to do it was to give her plenty of room and privacy.

Marge took time each day to teach Ann the African dialect. With the assistance of a notebook to help her remember, she made remarkable progress. Everyone seemed eager to help her learn the language. Paul would stand and laugh as the Africans pointed to their head, then their ears, eyes, mouths, teeth and tongues to help her. When she would say the word correctly, they would jump up and down and clap their hands.

"She sure has won their hearts," Ken said to Paul one day as they stood watching Ann taking care of her patients.

"Yes, she has," agreed Paul. "And . . . and if I don't watch out, she's going to win mine, too." The words were out before Paul realized it. Ken looked at him and smiled.

"I understand, Paul. It has been very lonely for you out here. I know you want the Lord's will for your life. I'll be praying for you, Paul. I surely will."

In a few weeks the new dispensary was finished. The gleaming aluminum roof and the concrete-block walls and floor made it an attraction for miles around. Chief Paul took off his shoes and walked barefoot across the cool, concrete veranda.

"The termites won't come up through that stuff," he said as he tapped his heel on the concrete. "We can't afford to let those little insects destroy any of this medicine. The Lord gave it to us for our people and not for those pesky little creatures."

Ann joined in the laughter of the others as Marge interpreted for her the village leader's amusing comments.

Chief Paul sent a message inviting Chief Ndeke to come to Yanga One and see the new dispensary. He came with several people and Chief Paul personally gave him a guided tour. He even had Ann demonstrate giving injections without the needle in the syringe.

"This lady is only here for a short time," Chief Paul told the visiting chief. "I think if we pray enough the Lord might give her to us to live here and be our nurse."

Ann asked Marge to translate for her so she would be sure of the chief's remarks. She smiled as Marge told her.

"I'm beginning to get the message that my African friends want me to stay," Ann told Marge after the two chiefs had gone from the building.

"They do want you to stay, Ann. We all want you to stay; but, of course, we want what the Lord wants."

Paul was extra careful about his relationship with Ann. He kept his distance as much as possible and still tried to be a good friend. One day he found her watching him as he was installing shuttered windows in the dispensary. She looked away as their eyes met and then glanced back at Paul. His heart skipped as her dark brown eyes met his again.

"How do you like your new window, Ann?" questioned Paul nervously.

"You missionaries seem to know how to do everything," answered the pretty nurse. "One day you're a preacher and the next a carpenter or maybe a mason."

"We have to be able to do those things, Ann, if we're going to get along out here."

"I think missionaries are the most unique people I know," continued Ann. "In fact, I think you are all just marvelous people. I love you all very much."

"And we love you, too, Ann," answered Paul, pretending to tighten a screw which was already in place. "You have become very special to us and are part of our family out here. We'll miss you terribly when you leave."

Paul felt awkward as he tried to converse with Ann and at the same time hide his true feelings for her.

"I'll miss you all, too," responded Ann. "I feel I belong here."

By the time her visit had ended, Ann had gained a special place in everyone's hearts. Chief Paul insisted that he host a big farewell party for her on behalf of the two villages.

"We'll come to Yanga Two and have the farewell," said the leader. "I will ride to the capital, too, when Dr. and Mrs. Simms take our sister to get her plane."

The setting of the farewell party was something to behold. Chief Paul had his men cut long bamboo poles with which they constructed arches over the mission driveway from the main road to the Simms's house—a distance of twelve hundred feet. The arches were then decorated with palm branches and colorful bougainvillea. Wild flowers were made into bouquets and tied to all the trees on the mission station. An open palm-leaf covered shelter was built for the special guests under which they could sit for protection from the hot sun. Chief Paul had his own personal, homemade chaise lounge brought from Yanga One for Ann Steele to use during the farewell party. The local administrator and his staff were invited as well as the chiefs in the surrounding area. By nine o'clock the morning of the big day, the mission station was jammed with people.

"I've never seen anything like this," said Marge as she left the house with Ken to join their African friends.

"All I can say," added Ken, "is that when Chief Paul does something, he does it well."

Paul Davis was scanning the crowd every now and then to see if he could spot the special guest for the day. As usual he found her with Chief Paul, who felt it was his responsibility to introduce Ann to as many people as he could, especially his fellow chiefs.

"I almost feel as though you are my daughter," Chief Paul said as he directed Ann to a group of village chiefs sitting under a wild fig tree. "You are really family to all of us, Miss Ann; so when you go back to your own country, I'm going to ask the Lord to make you so homesick for us that you will have to come back and live among us."

Ann smiled at the chief's remarks. Little did he realize that within her heart she was already seeking the mind of the Lord regarding a permanent return to Africa.

The women of Yanga One and the workmen's village at Yanga Two cooperated in preparing the food for the giant feast. The aroma of cooked manioc was in the air. As Paul made his way among his African friends, it seemed everywhere he turned someone was pushing food into his hands. Cooked plantain, sweet potatoes, dried meats and fish, roasted peanuts, peanut butter rolls, guavas, papayas and bananas were in abundance. The smell of strong coffee mingled with the scent of sour manioc told the story. A full-fledged African feast was in progress.

When all had eaten to their satisfaction, Chief Paul called for everyone to be quiet. He then mounted a small platform made for the occasion and asked the crowd to stand as Ken Simms read one of his favorite portions of Scripture, 1 Corinthians 15. Paul Davis led the several hundred people in the singing of a few hymns. Before Paul sat down, the village leader asked him to lead the group in singing "When the Roll Is Called Up Yonder." Ann Steele was then asked to say a few words. As she stood and faced the many Africans gathered on the mission station, her heart was deeply touched. Slowly she began to speak in her new language.

"I don't have the words to express the feelings of my heart today. I thank God for sending me to you. I thank Him for the privilege of serving Him in this wonderful place. I shall miss you all greatly. I will pray for you and if it is the Lord's will, someday I will return to be among you. Thank you all, and especially Chief Paul, for what you have done for me today."

With tears in her eyes and unable to speak any longer, Ann sat down. Chief Paul then asked Pastor Kondo to bring the message of the day from God's Word. At the close of the message, over seventy people stood to their feet to acknowledge that they were accepting Christ as their Savior. Ann Steele, thinking of her departure, was homesick already for her African friends.

Paul Davis again remained at Yanga Two while Ken and Marge Simms and Chief Paul accompanied the missionary nurse to the capital to get her plane. Just before Ann left Yanga Two, Paul asked for her address and told her that he would write and keep her informed of the happenings at the two Yangas.

The departure from the capital city was more difficult than anyone thought it would be. When her plane was announced, instead of the usual handshake, Chief Paul took her head lightly in his hands and blew gently into each of her ears. Ann had been among the Banda tribe long enough to know the meaning of this gesture.

"Thank you, Chief Paul," she said barely above a whisper. The lump in her throat made it nearly impossible for her to speak. Her eyes were filled with tears as she hugged Marge Simms and Dorothy Banks.

"You two are more like sisters than just co-workers. I've come to love you very much and I shall miss you terribly."

"We'll miss you, too," said Marge. "You have become such a part of our life and work out here that I don't know what we're going to do without you."

Ann shook hands with Ken and Dale and joined the other passengers who were on their way to board the DC-8. As the plane raced down the runway for takeoff, Ann wondered again if she would be returning to Africa someday.

18
A Double Wedding

The noise at the front door told Ann Steele that the postman had arrived. It had been three weeks since she had returned from Africa, and with each mail she was hoping there would be news from her missionary friends. Lifting the lid of the mailbox, Ann immediately caught sight of the foreign stamps. She quickly took the mail and slipped through the front door, sitting on the nearest chair. In the upper left-hand corner was the name "Paul Davis." Excitement gripped Ann as she nervously tore open the envelope.

"Dear Ann, It has been only hours since you left here. In fact, you are only partway to the Bible school station, but already I miss you more than words can tell. The past three months have been filled with happiness for all of us here at Yanga Two and Yanga One. I must confess to you, Ann, that the joy and happiness you have brought to my heart is the kind of happiness that I have greatly missed since the Lord took Becky Home to be with Him. Life alone out here can be very difficult at times. I did not share these thoughts with you while you were here, but the loneliness at times is almost unbearable. I don't know if I'm making very much sense with this letter, but I guess by now you are beginning to see that I miss you greatly and wish that it were possible for you to return."

As Ann continued reading Paul's letter, she was already forming in her mind her response to the man who had won a very special place in her heart. That evening, after much thinking, Ann responded to Paul's letter.

"I had been anxiously waiting to hear from you missionaries

and today your letter arrived. I enjoyed every moment of my time there in Africa. How I thank the Lord for directing me there this summer. I know you and I never discussed the Homegoing of your Becky or my Tom and little David, but I'm sure that we both look upon this as the Lord's will and we would not want to have it any other way.

"God has been working in my heart since I have arrived home. Last week I wrote to Dr. Lindsey and asked him what is required in order for me to apply to the mission. I have also discussed this with my pastor. He informed me that if God has called me to be a missionary, my home church will take on my full support. At this point, I don't have peace to think of any other thing than to return to Africa. I ask you to pray for me that the Lord's will be done. That is my desire and I know it is your desire for me, too.

"I must confess, Paul, that there were many times that I wanted to talk with you; but I realized that with both of us being single, we had to be very careful in our actions before our African brothers and sisters. You mentioned in your letter that you missed me. I miss you, too, and I am hoping that you will keep the correspondence coming, informing me of what's taking place at the two Yangas."

The next morning Ann slipped the letter in the mailbox on the corner, convinced that Paul would gladly receive it.

Not realizing how much Ann Steele was in his conversation, Paul soon became the target of Ken's teasing.

"What's the cost for a pound of airmail to Indianapolis, Paul?" joked Ken one night at the dinner table.

"Now, why would you ask me that?" asked Paul, smiling.

"Well, the way you keep writing those letters every night, you'll have a pound of them by the time the mail goes out."

"Don't listen to him, Paul," chimed in Marge. "I think she's a very lovely girl. If it takes a pound of letters each week to win her, then I'd say it's a good investment."

A few days letter the mail sack arrived with a letter from Ann. Paul disappeared into his bedroom while he read the letter over and over again. There was no mistake about it—Paul Davis was in love with Ann Steele and he hoped that Ann felt the same about him. When the mail sack left the post the next day for the capital, there were three letters inside destined for the city of Indianapolis, Indiana.

Two times each week, Pastor Kondo traveled the twenty miles to Yanga One and preached in the village chapel. To assist the pastor in this ministry, Paul or Ken would drive his pickup, making the trip much easier for their African brother. Now and then, Chief Paul would ride back to Yanga Two with them. Whenever he did, the missionaries would hold their breath to see if he was bringing his little basket containing his favorite food—cooked manioc with caterpillar sauce.

In Ann's third letter to Paul, she told him that she loved him. She also gave him the good news that with her nurse's degree and her three years of Bible correspondence courses, plus one year of evening Bible institute there in Indianapolis, all her educational requirements for acceptance by the mission were met. She had formally applied, had received her preliminary papers, completed them and returned them. The Candidate Secretary had written to inform her that there was a possibility she could appear before the General Council of the mission in March the following spring, and attend Candidate Seminar for two weeks in July. If all went well, that would make her an authorized missionary by August 1.

Paul's next letter to Ann was both difficult and exciting to write. As he wrote, he asked the Lord to give him just the right words to say.

"Praise the Lord for the wonderful news of your last letter. Telling me you love me has made me a very happy man. Chief Paul is here. When I told him that you had applied to the mission to come out here as a missionary, he shouted for joy. Tonight was prayer meeting here at Yanga Two and Pastor Kondo shared the good news with the church family of your call to Africa. Many cried for joy. We all love you, Ann, and we're anxious for you to return."

Paul struggled for just the right words as he continued. "You mentioned that our Candidate Secretary wrote and said there is a possibility for you to appear before the General Council in March for your oral, doctrinal examination. By the way, I didn't know you had taken correspondence studies and had a year of Bible institute work there in Indianapolis. Something tells me there are many good things about you that we don't know.

"After you pass your examination in March, you will have only your Candidate Seminar and then will be free to come to the field. This brings me to another important matter. The Lord willing, there will be a wedding ceremony here next summer. As you know, Tene and Ruth plan to marry. I'm sure that with a little persuasion, they would wait until the month of August. What I am proposing, Ann, is since your church plans to provide your full support, why don't you come immediately to the field and we could make it a double wedding ceremony? I know this will be a surprise to you, but we love each other and God has called us to work here in Africa. I love you, Ann, and I want you to marry me."

After Paul had written his proposal, he bowed his head and committed his letter to the Lord. He would take it to the post the next morning to be placed in the mail sack for the capital.

That night the Simmses and Paul enjoyed the company of Chief Paul and Pastor and Mrs. Kondo. The six friends talked long into the night, recounting the blessings of the Lord there in the work among the Banda tribe. They were just saying good night when they heard the terrible death wail.

19

Another Preaching Post

"That's the death wail!" called Chief Paul, running to look out the front door. "They're coming down the driveway. I can see four lanterns."

Ken grabbed a nearby flashlight and ran down the drive to meet the wailing Africans.

"What's wrong?" he called as he got near the group.

"It's my daughter," cried a woman who was walking beside a crude stretcher made from a blanket fastened over two poles. The two men carrying the poles stopped and placed their motionless passenger on the ground. The medical doctor made a quick examination of the young girl.

"What is it, Ken?" asked Paul, kneeling beside his co-worker. "Is she dead?"

"Not yet," answered Ken. "There's a slight pulse but it is very weak. She needs blood and she needs it now. Marge! Take Kondo, Chief Paul and Paul to the dispensary. I need to know their blood types. We'll get a sample from this girl, too. She's bleeding badly from the gash in her leg. We must act quickly."

Using his handerchief as a tourniquet, Ken had the men carry the girl to the dispensary. "The only thing that saved her life is that her mother put pressure on the wound, which cut down the flow of blood."

"This is the witch doctor's daughter from Bissi," said Kondo. "He was to return today from the Yondo ceremonies he is conducting out in the jungles."

While Marge checked for the blood types, Ken worked feverishly with the young girl's wound. "Her mother says that the girl is their only daughter. Her father has already promised her to be the wife of another witch doctor near Yanga One," said Kondo.

"But she's only a child," added Paul. "I don't think she's any more than ten years old."

Just then a man came running into the dispensary. "Where is she? Where's my daughter? Is she dead?"

Chief Paul grabbed the distraught father by the shoulder. "Your daughter is not dead, Sioni. Stop your yelling. Dr. Simms is taking good care of her."

"How did she do this?" asked Ken of several Africans from the village of Bissi.

"She was cutting wood with an ax and it slipped and hit her in the leg," said one of the men.

"Paul's blood matches," spoke Marge, coming out of the lab.

"Great! Draw a pint, Marge," said her husband. "We have to get some blood into this girl as soon as possible."

Ken kept working on the girl as he spoke. When the Africans saw Paul crawl up on the table to give blood, they gasped. Some of them covered their mouths with their hands as Marge put the needle in and the blood began filling a small plastic bag.

"That's his life you're taking," said one of the older men.

"What are you doing to him?" questioned the girl's father. "He will die."

"No, he won't die," answered Ken. "Mr. Davis has the same kind of blood as your daughter. She has lost a lot of her blood, and if she doesn't get more very soon she could die. Mr. Davis is giving her some of his blood."

"He's what?" blurted out the witch doctor. "How can he do that? You can't put blood back into a person."

"Yes, I can," answered Ken confidently. "If I couldn't, then your daughter would surely die."

Knowing the strange religious beliefs of the Banda tribe about blood, Ken wanted to major on the fact that the girl needed the blood in order to live. He knew that none of the non-Christians would give theirs. He was even surprised that Chief Paul and Pastor Kondo had submitted to blood-typing without question.

In a short time Ken had tied off the severed veins. The young girl was placed on a table where the bag of blood was fastened above her. The girl's father seemed to be in a trance as he watched the missionary's blood drip into the tube and needle that led into his daughter's arm.

"I've never seen anything like this," said the astonished father. "My heart is overwhelmed to think that this white man of God would do this for someone he doesn't know."

"It's because his heart is filled with love for our people," responded Chief Paul. "You just returned from the Yondo ceremonies where you and your helpers cut tribal designs into the bodies of young people—young people just like your daughter. You've taught them how to make blood sacrifices and encouraged them to worship unknown gods."

The entire room was silent as the African chief spoke. No one would dare to interrupt Chief Paul. The witch doctor stared at the trickling blood as the chief continued.

"These missionaries have come to give us good words about the only true God. He is a God Who loves us but hates our sin. The message from His Book tells us how He loved us so much that He gave His only Son, Jesus, to die in our place for our sins. He shed His blood for all of us, my fellow tribesmen, so we wouldn't have to pay the penalty of our sins. Because Jesus died, we can live forever."

"You mean that the God you speak about loves me and that His Son died for me, too?" asked the witch doctor incredulously.

"That's right," answered Chief Paul. "Sioni, you can have everlasting life if you will confess your sins to God and accept His Son, Jesus, as your Savior."

"But you said Jesus died. How can He do anything for me now?"

"Because He came back from the dead," continued Chief Paul. "You see, because He is God, death could not hold Him. He conquered death for all who will accept Him. My brother Kota, whom you all knew, accepted Jesus just before he died. Hear me, my friends, Kota is not really in the ground. That's only his body. His soul is in Heaven which is God's village. Kota and I will live forever with Jesus in Heaven."

The witch doctor continued to sit as though in deep thought. He leaned forward as his daughter opened her eyes.

"She's alive! She sees me!" he cried.

"Mr. Davis's blood is giving her strength," said Pastor Kondo. "God is answering our prayers."

"You mean that you have been asking your God to help my daughter live?" The witch doctor was overwhelmed with the love and concern of the Christians. "Why didn't I know about all this kindness before now?"

"Because you wouldn't let any of us who know God talk to you about Him. Pastor Kondo has been chased from your village many times. You wouldn't allow us to show any love and kindness to you and the people of your village."

The witch doctor hung his head in shame. "I see it all now," he said. "I can see your God's love through each of you. I have been blind. It took this terrible happening to my daughter for me to hear you."

"You've known me for many years," Chief Paul continued. "You knew me when I fulfilled my previous name, 'Ngonjo.' "

"And wicked and mean you were, Chief," added Sioni, laughing nervously. "I knew something happened to you, but I thought you were just trying to be nice so you would get the missionaries to build you that house of medicine I heard about."

"I can't be nice in myself," continued the African leader. "Jesus did it all for me. He made the change in my life and He can do the same in your life, Sioni."

Chief Paul finally stood up and asked everyone in the room to bow their heads and close their eyes. Marge stood attentively beside the witch doctor's daughter. Ken wondered what Chief Paul was going to do.

"Your daughter is going to live, Sioni. Our God has spared her life. Now what about all these good words we've been talking about here in this room? Are you going to close your heart to them?"

The witch doctor slowly shook his head, indicating he would not. He lifted his head and looked at Chief Paul. "I want what you have, Ngonjo . . . uh . . . uh . . . Paul. My heart is troubled. I want your God to make it well. I want to be happy like you and Pastor Kondo and these missionaries."

During the next few moments Chief Paul assisted Sioni in praying. He stood up to show his respect to God and slowly but clearly confessed his sinfulness and asked Jesus to save him. As Sioni prayed, other voices could be heard praying the same prayer. Seven men and three women, including Sioni and his wife, accepted Jesus as their Savior. Paul said he would stay in the dispensary that night with the girl and her parents. The Simmses and Chief Paul returned to the mission house. Kondo stayed to talk and pray with the new converts and then returned to the workmen's village. Before they retired, Ken and Marge talked with Chief Paul about the conversion of the ten people from Bissi.

"That village will give us another preaching post in this district," spoke the African excitedly. "Why, with so many believers there, maybe someday a church can be started."

"But who is going to pastor these new churches, Chief Paul?" asked Ken, hoping the enthusiastic leader would really see the problem.

"We need to challenge our young men, Dr. Simms. That's what we need to do. We need to challenge the young men of Good News and Yanga One and Bissi." The village leader hesitated and then spoke out again. He drove his fist into his open hand as he talked. "Pastor Kondo and Tene can't do the job alone. They need help and help they will get. Dr. Simms, let's pray now. Let's dedicate ourselves to the task of reaching our Banda young men. If I were younger I would go to Bible school, but since I can't go I want to do all I can to discover those whom God wants to serve Him that way.

Later on when they were alone, Ken and Marge discussed Chief Paul's remarks.

"What a spiritual giant he is turning out to be," said Ken. "I have the feeling that we are going to see some new men from this area in Bible school in the next couple of years."

Unknown to Ken and Marge, Chief Paul was on his knees beside his bed that very moment, asking God if there was something he could do to encourage the young men to go to Bible school.

20
Congratulations, Paul

During the month following the serious accident of the former witch doctor's daughter, many things took place in the region of Yanga One and Yanga Two. With the help of Chief Paul, Sioni announced there would be a burning of his witchcraft material and invited anyone who wanted to see it to come. Several hundred people made their way to the village of Bissi to watch the converted witch doctor defy the gods he once worshiped.

Pastor Kondo was on hand to help with the burning. A huge pile of masks, bones and boxes was set on fire with the aid of some gasoline provided by Paul Davis. As the flames leaped higher, the Christians in the group joined their voices in singing, "What can wash away my sins? Nothing but the blood of Jesus."

After the fire was nearly burned out, the witch doctor asked for the attention of the crowd and announced that from then on he didn't want to be called Sioni any longer, since that meant "wickedness." Chief Paul had told him that John the disciple was close to Jesus and the converted witch doctor knew immediately that that described his feelings. From now on he was to be called "John."

Chief Paul called Chief Ndeke, John, Pastor Kondo, Ken and Paul to a special meeting at Yanga One. For one full day they planned how they would unite their efforts to reach as many of the villages as possible with the gospel. One of their goals was to challenge Christian young men for the need of more pastors and evangelists.

It was four weeks after the accident that Ken, Marge and Paul stopped off at Bissi to see John's daughter. She was sitting in front of her father's hut when the blue pickup drove into the village.

"Hello, Katcha!" called Ken, stepping down from the cab. "I've come to check on that leg." The young girl stood and reached out her hand for the usual handshake.

"It feels good, Dr. Simms. It doesn't hurt when I walk now."

Katcha's mother appeared from the hut and immediately shook hands with the visitors. "My husband is out in the peanut garden. If you wish, I can send someone for him."

"Oh, no," said Ken, "that won't be necessary. We have to make another stop so we can't stay long."

Before they left, they were served some roasted peanuts and black coffee. Paul never did get used to the strong African coffee, but for the sake of a good relationship with the Africans he always managed to drink it. On their arrival at the mission station, they met one of the administrator's men with the mail delivery.

"This isn't the day for the mail to come," said Paul as he got out of the truck to take the bag from the porter.

"I know it isn't, Mr. Davis," replied the African, "but a visiting administrator arrived from the capital today and went by the post office before he left. He picked up the mail for our post."

Ken and Marge sensed Paul's excitement when they reached the house. He had not heard from Ann in two weeks and she had had time to reply to his proposal. As the bag was emptied on the dining room table, Paul spotted the familiar handwriting immediately. He took the letter and retreated to a nearby chair to read it. Ken and Marge continued to sort the other pieces of mail.

"My Dearest Paul." Paul's heart beat hard as he read on. "I received your letter a week ago asking me to marry you. All this week I have waited upon the Lord before I wrote back. I'm sorry if I have caused you any anxiety, but I wanted to give myself this time to pray about it. My answer is yes. I love you and would be honored to be your wife."

"Praise the Lord!" called Paul excitedly. "Ann says she will marry me."

"Congratulations, Paul," said Ken, striding over to shake his co-worker's hand. "She's a wonderful girl."

That night Paul wrote a letter to Tene, asking him if he would put off his marriage to Ruth until the month of August. "If all goes well," he wrote, "Mrs. Steele and I will be getting married that month. I think it would be nice if we could have a double wedding ceremony. Please let me hear from you regarding this request."

News of Paul's planned marriage to the short-term nurse spread quickly among the Christians. Tentative plans were for Pastor Kondo and Ken Simms to have part in the ceremony. Tene wrote and said that if it was all right with Ruth, he would be happy to postpone their marriage a month or so.

Meanwhile, Ann Steele continued her correspondence with the mission agency. The Candidate Secretary wrote and told her that her references were received in better than average time, and it looked as if he would be able to present her preliminary application in the next meeting of the Candidate Committee, which was one week away.

Just two weeks later Ann received a thick envelope from the mission agency. Inside was a letter telling her that her preliminary application was approved and the enclosed doctrinal papers were for her to complete before the March conference. This gave her several weeks and she was sure she could get them done with time to spare. In her letter to Paul she mentioned that she was going to try and complete her doctrinal papers by the end of January.

As Ann worked on her doctrinal papers, exciting things were happening at the village of Good News. Chief Paul and Pastor Kondo made a trip to the village at Chief Ndeke's request. Pastor Kondo brought a message on Christian service from Romans 12:1. At the close of the message, three teenage boys stood up declaring themselves candidates for Bible school. Two of them had been saved the first time Chief Paul had spoken there. The third one had accepted Christ one evening in his hut after hearing Chief Ndeke give his testimony.

"Praise the Lord," said Chief Paul as he shook hands with the young men. "I'm inviting you to come and live at Yanga One at my expense. We have reading and writing classes there. Pastor Kondo will also teach you from God's Word. By September of next year you should be ready to go to Bible school."

The three young men were so anxious to begin their training that they left with Chief Paul and Pastor Kondo two days later.

During the two days of travel, Chief Paul insisted that the men begin memorizing Scripture. Directed by Kondo who read the verses aloud, the party memorized the first three chapters of the Gospel of John by the time they arrived at Yanga One. Chief Paul asked several of his men to work with the three men from Good News and help them build houses. The village leader had the men clear a piece of ground located between the village and where his mother, Bio, had lived before she was saved. He went with Kondo several days later to inspect the new site.

"Do you know what I see out there in that area, Kondo?"

Never knowing what Chief Paul was going to come up with, the African pastor replied hesitantly. "No, I don't know what you see, Chief Paul."

The chief raised his hand, motioning toward the large clearing where three homes were being constructed. "I see houses,—lots of houses. And Kondo, they are all filled with Bible school students. Why can't we develop a pre-Bible school here at Yanga One? Yes, a preparation school for those who need this basic training. This could be our Bible students' village. Why there must be space out there for fifteen houses. What do you think of it, Kondo? Do you think it can be done?"

The more the pastor thought about it, the more exciting it all sounded. "I think it's a wonderful idea, Chief Paul. Yanga One could be the pre-Bible school training center for all the villages in our district. I would say there are at least fifty in our district."

When Pastor Kondo returned to Yanga Two, he shared Chief Paul's suggestion with the missionaries.

"What a man!" said Ken. "This has been one big miracle—from the time Paul and I were chased from Chief Paul's village to now. And we continue to see things happen every day."

"It's been a wonderful experience," added Paul. "I thank God that He has privileged me to be a part of it. I know there are some great things ahead for all of us."

Paul then excused himself. He went to his room and got out his writing paper. Not only might Ann work in the dispensary at Yanga One, but there was also the possibility that she and Paul would be assisting Kondo or Tene in the pre-Bible school. His heart was filled as he penned his thoughts to Ann of the future of the work.

21

Car Trouble

By the time January rolled around, Pastor Kondo had more than he could handle at the villages of Yanga One, Yanga Two, Bissi and Good News. Four more young men had moved to Yanga One for pre-Bible school training and that ministry alone was demanding more and more of his time. Chief Paul was helping where he could, but he realized his lack of Bible school training and mentioned that he just might pack up some day and go to Bible school.

The news from Marie indicated that she was enjoying Bible college. She was delighted to find her name listed in the top half of the class at the end of her first semester. In her letters to Ken and Marge, she kept them posted as to what was taking place with Henry Duval and his unsaved wife. They had visited her at school and could not get over the fact that there were such clean-living young people in the world. Their love and dedication to the Lord made such an impression on Mrs. Duval that she mentioned it to Marie at least four times. When they left, they promised to return soon. Marie requested that the missionaries pray for the Duvals.

Paul's correspondence with Ann Steele continued. The latest letter from her spoke of a March interview with the mission council.

"Mr. Large wrote and said he has gone over my doctrinal papers and everything seems to be in order. He has scheduled me to appear before the council the second week of March."

The many medical cases kept Ken Simms busy from morning to night. His trips to Yanga One became fewer and fewer. The new dispensary building had been finished for several months, but there just weren't enough medical personnel to man it. Chief Paul became more and more concerned for the needs of the Banda people.

"Isn't there something we can do, Dr. Simms?" he asked Ken one day. "We need a nurse for our dispensary and a teacher for our pre-Bible school."

Ken explained to Chief Paul that Ann was scheduled to appear before the mission council in March and that her candidate training would be over at the end of July. "That's only six months, Chief Paul. Her church is going to help her with funds so she doesn't have to travel to other churches seeking support as most of the missionaries have to do. Some missionaries travel for two to three years before they have enough funds to go to the mission field."

"But we can build a house for anyone who wants to come here. My people can provide food for them, too."

Ken then explained further to the chief how the missionaries must have funds to pay their plane or ship transportation, and also if they need a vehicle they have to buy that with their funds as well. When he finished, the African shook his hand, snapping his fingers.

"Well, like I said, we can build the missionaries' houses and supply them with food, but I can see that is only part of their need."

Ken shook hands with the chief as he saw Pastor Kondo coming out of the chapel. "I had better be going, Chief Paul. I see Kondo is through with his class and I promised my wife I would come home as soon as I could. Rev. and Mrs. Banks are coming today. Their letter said they were to stay at the Bible school station last night and they should be arriving about now."

The African chief shook hands firmly with his missionary friend. "Give my greetings to Mr. and Mrs. Banks. If they stay long enough, perhaps you can invite me to your house so I can treat you with another special Banda meal."

"Thank you, Chief," said Ken, remembering the manioc and caterpillar sauce. "I'll mention that to my wife and the Banks."

Ken was surprised when he arrived home and found that the Banks had not yet arrived. "They must have had car trouble along the way. Surely they should be here by now."

Marge had the food ready and waiting for the arrival of their co-workers. "What do you think we should do, Ken? They should have been here long before now."

"We'll just have to wait," answered Ken. "I suppose I could go meet them, but that would leave you here alone. If Paul were here, I'm sure he would go looking for them."

"He's probably sitting around a fire at Good News with Chief Ndeke right now," spoke Ken. "The Africans love to do that at this time of night."

As the evening wore on, Ken and Marge became increasingly concerned. They decided they might as well eat since there was no way of knowing when Dale and Dorothy would arrive. At nine o'clock, Ken told Marge to pack a basket with food and water. "Let's take some hot coffee along, too. I'm certain something has happened to them."

The worried doctor went to the dispensary and carefully chose a supply of medicines and materials to take with him. While there, he checked his patients and gave some last-minute instructions to his African helper. He had notified several of the workmen from the village that he wanted them to go with him. By the time he arrived at the pickup, they had already filled the tank with gas and had four five-gallon cans of gas in the back. Ken checked to make sure there were a couple of shovels, axes and a coil of rope in the truck. Marge brought several blankets, flashlights and extra batteries.

"You would think we were going on a long trip," mused Ken, "but then traveling in the heart of Africa at night can be dangerous. One never knows what to expect."

"Especially in a case like tonight," added Marge.

Between them on the seat was a supply of chocolate bars which they had purchased at the capital their last trip. They kept them on hand for a special treat now and then, but Marge thought the men in the back of the truck would enjoy them as they rode in the cold night air.

Pastor Kondo, who came to help pack the truck, led in prayer before the group left. "Father, we have come to You for many things in the past. Now I'm committing these loved ones to You. Be with them as they travel. Give them safety on the road. And, Lord, help them find Mr. and Mrs. Banks unharmed."

As the pastor finished his prayer, the men echoed his "amen."

The Bible school village was a good eight-hour drive because of the condition of the road. Ken held the steering wheel tightly as he swerved to avoid the holes and rocks in the road. As they rounded each turn, they expected to find their co-workers. They had traveled for two hours when they saw a man on a bicycle ahead. He was waving his arms frantically. Ken stopped beside the man, who began talking with the men in the truck.

"Two white people had an accident with their car. It ran off the road," spoke the man excitedly.

"Are they hurt?" asked Ken.

"The man hurt his hand. I saw blood on his clothes," answered the messenger.

"How far are they?" questioned Ken, checking his reading on the odometer.

"I probably have been traveling long enough for the sun to travel from there to there." The man pointed to where the sun would be at about two o'clock and then five o'clock.

"That's probably about an hour's ride yet," said Ken, roughly figuring the comparison of a bicycle's time against that of his truck.

The cyclist was so excited about giving the information to the search party that he forgot to give them the note he had in his pocket from Dorothy. Ken gave the man some money and they continued on their way in search of the accident victims.

It was just about an hour later that they sighted a fire beside the road.

"It's them!" shouted Marge. "There's Dorothy . . . and . . . and . . . there's Dale, too."

Ken brought the truck to a stop and in seconds everyone was running toward the two missionaries. "Boy are we ever glad to see you," shouted Dale, slapping at the mosquitoes. "We're just about eaten alive."

"Are you all right?" asked Ken, taking a look at Dale's hand. He had tied a handerchief around it to keep the insects away.

"Oh, it's nothing, Ken. My tie-rod broke and we were off the road before we knew it. I tried to fix it and cut my hand a little."

The doctor looked at Dale's hand as Marge held the light. "It probably should have some stitches, Dale. I'm going to tape it for now. When we get back to the station, I'll have another look at it. I am going to give you a tetanus shot, however."

After caring for his co-worker, Ken and his men went to look at the car. Without even telling the men what to do, they went to work, jacking up the front of the car and blocking it with large wooden blocks that they had brought with them. In minutes the men had the wheels straight and had very carefully fitted the damaged tie-rod end together.

Ken smiled as he saw one of the men pull several long inch-wide pieces of inner tubing out of the back of the truck. "Well, there's old faithful," he said to Dale, pointing to the straps. "I've seen those straps used for many purposes."

The men took the straps and, one at a time, pulled them tight and wrapped them around the steering knuckle. When they were finished, they had a ball of rubber as big as a grapefruit.

"That will do it, Dr. Simms," said one of the men. "It won't come loose now."

Ken fastened a chain to his front axle and, with the men pushing, Dale's car was soon back on the road.

"Ken," said Dale, "if you don't mind, will you take Dorothy with you and Marge? I'll take your men in the car with me. That way, they'll be warm."

Dale took the lead and Ken followed with the pickup. It was necessary for him to stay far enough behind so he wouldn't get Dale's dust.

"Praise the Lord, Dorothy, that neither of you were seriously hurt," spoke Ken as they started home.

"It happened so quickly. We were off the road before we knew it," responded Dorothy. "Then an African came by on a bicycle and we gave him a note for you. Did you see him?"

"We met a man on a bicycle, but he didn't give us a note," Marge answered. "What did it say?"

"I wrote that our tie-rod end had broken and we were off the road. Dale estimated how far we were from Yanga Two. I also said to bring food and water *and* mosquito repellant."

The three missionaries laughed, thankful that nothing serious had happened to anyone and that the car's problem was only a minor one. Their laughter would no doubt have subsided to silence and prayer had they known what their co-worker, Paul Davis, was going through at that very moment.

22

Malaria

Paul Davis knew something was wrong. Just before he was scheduled to eat lunch with Chief Ndeke, he began having chills. His entire body ached and he had difficulty focusing his eyes. He grew worse by the minute.

It was a struggle for him to get off the camp cot and stand up. As he tried to walk, his legs seemed like rubber bands. He staggered to the door of the hut and headed for Chief Ndeke's house some fifty yards away. The hot tropical sun beat hard upon him. Something inside him told him to keep going, even though he wanted to lie down right there on the path.

"I've . . . I've got to keep going," Paul stammered. "Not far now. I've got to make it."

The missionary lifted his eyes to see how much farther he had to walk. The huts seemed to blend into one big blurr. He tried to focus on the people, but they faded in and out of his vision.

"Help . . . help . . . help me!" called Paul in a feeble voice. He knew he was falling, but fought to stay on his feet.

Chief Ndeke sat in his chaise lounge in front of his hut. He was pleased to have the missionary come and visit him and his people. To show his appreciation, he had planned a large feast for the evening. For the noon meal, however, the village chief had invited Paul to eat sweet potatoes and fish sauce with him. The chief looked up just in time to see Paul come out of his hut and head for his house. The village leader noticed that Paul was not walking straight. Several times he thought Paul would fall, but the missionary always managed to regain his balance and continue. When Paul got just about halfway, he lifted his head and called for help. At the same time he fell heavily to the ground.

Chief Ndeke jumped to his feet and called for someone to go help the missionary. In seconds the chief was standing beside his missionary friend. "Take him into my house. Maybe the heat is too much for him."

"His body is very hot, Chief. He does not see or speak. Mr. Davis is very sick," said one of the older men.

Within minutes they had carried Paul into the chief's hut and laid him on the leader's bed. Meanwhile, Chief Ndeke asked for the only two bicycles in the village of Good News. He told the owners to tell Chief Paul about the missionary's illness and for him to send word to Dr. Simms. By sending two messengers, the chief wanted to be sure that the word would arrive, that it would arrive in good time, and that it would be accurate.

"Get me some water in a clay pot," demanded the chief. The condensation that takes place with a clay pot tends to keep the water cool inside, and just now Paul needed a cool, damp cloth on his head. He had learned this from Chief Paul, who had watched Dr. and Mrs. Simms do this with patients with high fevers.

Paul began to toss on the bed, calling out to Ken Simms. "That's where we'll build it, Ken. There it is over there. You can see it. Now it's coming. Look out, Ken! Look out!"

"He's not talking straight," said Chief Ndeke as he placed the damp cloth on Paul's head. Two of the men held the delirious missionary so he wouldn't knock the cloth off his head. Chief Ndeke dipped the cloth into a bowl of water every few minutes in order to keep it cool. In a short while, Paul opened his eyes. He looked around, seemingly confused.

"Hello, Chief Ndeke. Where am I? Am I late for lunch?"

"You're not well, Mr. Davis. You fell coming over to my house. I've sent for Dr. Simms."

"I think I know what it is, Chief Ndeke," spoke the ill missionary. "It's malaria. I've been taking anti-malarial pills, but evidently I wasn't taking enough." Paul reached up to feel the wet cloth on his head. "This is good thinking, Chief. I know I must have been delirious. That cool cloth must have brought me out of it."

Paul motioned feebly toward the door. "I have medicine in my suitcase, Chief. If one of your men will go over and get it, I can give myself an injection of an anti-malarial drug."

Paul had the bag within minutes. He opened a vial and filled a syringe with the vaccine. Slowly he injected the drug into his hip. Chief Ndeke and the other men cringed as they saw the needle penetrate Paul's body. Within an hour Paul was asleep. Chief Ndeke insisted they leave him alone in the hut but ordered one of the men to sit in the doorway.

That night the feast was cancelled. The guest was ill with malaria and needed their prayers more than their food.

It was about midnight when the two men arrived at Yanga One with the message about Paul. Chief Paul immediately dispatched two of his cyclists on to Yanga Two. After the men left, the village leader called the Christians together to pray for Paul. Even Chief Paul smiled when he heard the prayer of one of the older men who had received Christ only a few months before.

"Lord," he prayed, "You know all about us. You knew when those mosquitoes were biting Mr. Davis that they would make him sick. Why, You could have stopped them from doing it, but You didn't. All I can think of is that there is a big reason why You allowed Mr. Davis to become sick. Help our two men to get to Yanga Two right away. It's so dark out there. Don't let any snakes get tangled in their bicycle wheels." Several of the men snickered. "Now the last thing I'm asking You, Lord, is this. It doesn't feel good to be sick. Mr. Davis is sick and he's a long way from Dr. Simms. You're a doctor, too, Lord, so I'm asking You to treat Mr. Davis for whatever is wrong with him."

In an hour, the two men rode into the mission station at Yanga Two. To their surprise, the Simmses were not there. A man hired to watch the property told them that Dr. and Mrs. Simms went looking for Mr. and Mrs. Banks and he had no idea when they would return. The two men sat down on the front veranda to wait for the missionaries.

Marge jerked her head up as it dropped to one side, touching Ken's shoulder. "I can hardly stay awake," she said, rubbing her eyes. "I'll sure be ready for bed when we get home."

"What time is it?" asked Ken, staring hard at the road and the two taillights in the distance. "We must be getting close to the post."

"It's nearly four o'clock," answered Marge, holding her wrist close to the dashboard lights so she could see her watch.

"Oh, the life of a missionary in the heart of Africa," breathed Dorothy. "But we all love it, don't we?"

In another half-hour the two vehicles arrived at the mission station. They had gone about halfway down the driveway when the headlights revealed the two men from Yanga One standing beside the house.

"Who are those men?" questioned Marge.

"They probably brought someone who is sick," responded Ken. "I don't think there's a night goes by now that someone doesn't come. This must be a bad time for malaria. There is sure a lot of it around."

Dale pulled into the backyard by the garage while Ken parked beside the house. The two Africans quickly approached the truck.

"Why they're from Yanga One," said Ken, stepping down from the cab. "I wonder if something has happened to Chief Paul."

"Hello, Dr. Simms. Chief Paul sent us. We have some bad news about Mr. Davis."

"What is it?" questioned Ken.

"Yesterday when the sun was overhead like this," the men pointed to the sky directly overhead, "Mr. Davis was supposed to eat with Chief Ndeke. On his way to the chief's house, he fell to the ground and was carried into the chief's hut."

"Yes, go on," said Ken, anxious to hear the rest of the report. "Then what happened?"

"We don't know, Dr. Simms. This is all the message given to us by the two messengers from Good News. They must have been sent out immediately after Mr. Davis became ill."

"What are we going to do, Ken?" asked Marge. "Good News is two days' travel by foot from Yanga One."

"I'm going to go by bicycle," responded Ken. "Paul could be very seriously ill. In fact, he could. . . ." Ken never finished the sentence. He regretted he had said that much. They all knew their minds were tired from the sleepless night and they weren't alert in their thinking.

Although he had been nearly twenty-four hours without sleep, the missionary doctor realized that a co-worker was in critical need of medical attention. The thought of the possible situation gave new strength to Ken. It was decided that Dale would stay at Yanga Two with Dorothy and Marge. Ken would drive his pickup as far as Yanga One, and from there travel by bicycle with several Africans accompanying him to Good News. If he could leave Yanga One within the next hour, he was sure he could be in Good News by late afternoon or evening.

Within thirty minutes he was driving the pickup hard toward Yanga One. His co-worker's life could be hanging in the balance and he must spend every effort to reach him.

23

Tragedy at Good News

The people of Good News greeted their chief's announcements with handclapping and cheers. Mr. Davis was feeling much better and was even able to drink some beef broth which the chief's wife had made for him. By noon the next day he was able to leave the hut and sit in a chaise lounge. It was while Paul was sitting there alone that Nasara approached him.

"Hello, Mr. Davis," spoke the young man. "I see you are much better."

"Yes, I'm feeling a lot better, uh . . . uh," Paul tried to think of the African's name.

"Nasara!" said the African. "My name is Nasara."

"That's right," exclaimed the missionary. "How could I forget? You were one of the men we met on the path that day when Pastor Kondo and I came to your village with Chief Paul."

"I should have killed you then," Nasara sneered in a voice so low none of the other villagers could hear him. "You have divided our village with that Book you carry with you—that Book you say comes from God."

Paul was stunned. Was his visitor serious or just playing a joke? The look in Nasara's eyes, however, soon convinced the missionary that he meant every word he said.

"I . . . I don't understand, Nasara," Paul responded hesitantly. His body stiffened as his eyes met the African's intense stare.

"I'll tell you now, White Man, I'm out to hurt you. You have fooled most everyone in this village, including our chief. He even changed the name of this village because of you. Three of our men are living in Yanga One because you intruded in their private lives."

Nasara stopped speaking as one of the villagers passed by. "I know you won't report me to the others. According to your own words, you want only to help us. That would not help me and you know it."

The young man reached into a sack he had slung over his shoulder. Slowly he pulled an arrow out far enough so Paul could see the point. "You see this arrow, Mr. Davis? Well, there are ten more in the sack. Every one has poison on the tip. I made them for you."

A chill ran up Paul's spine. "But . . . but why me?" asked the missionary, still confused over Nasara's attitude.

"I told you why," answered the African. "You have defied the gods of our fathers with your white man's religion. I thought the mambas would kill you and your *friend* [he spat the word out] when you came before, but you escaped."

"You mean Pastor Kondo?"

"That's the one," whispered Nasara as another villager passed by. "He's no Banda anymore. He's a white man like you."

Nasara turned to leave and then faced Paul again. "I'm leaving now, Mr. Davis, but you will know that I'm around. You see, my gods won't fail me. When one of these arrows strikes you, you will die. I'm going to dig your grave."

Nasara disappeared as quickly as he had come. Paul was overwhelmed. Never had he heard anything like that. He knew there were some bitter people in the village of Good News, but he had no idea one of them would threaten his life.

"You know all about this, Father," Paul said in a whisper as he thought out loud. He was happy to see Chief Ndeke returning from an inspection of a nearby cotton garden. Suddenly Paul was afraid. He thought of the threat of death hanging over his head and the terrible agony one could go through from the poison. He had seen animals shot with poison arrows. He recalled how he always felt sorry for them as he watched them slowly die. Was he to die that way? Paul tried to push the thoughts out of his mind.

"Hello, Mr. Davis," called Chief Ndeke. "You must be feeling better."

"I am, thank you," responded Paul, wondering if he should say anything to the chief about Nasara.

"Even though you may feel better, you are still a sick man, Mr. Davis. If my calculations are correct, Dr. Simms could arrive any time now. I'm sure he will come from Yanga One by bicycle."

Paul soon returned to his bed inside the chief's house and in a few minutes was sound asleep. Every now and then Chief Ndeke looked inside to check on his special visitor. It didn't seem possible that this man sleeping in his house was the same one he had told to leave his village and never come back.

The sun had just reached the top of the distant hills when Ken Simms and the men arrived. Ken went immediately to the chief's hut to see his co-worker. He was pleased to find Paul looking so well—much better than the doctor had expected.

"It's a good thing you had some injections with you, Paul. Had you not been alert enough to give yourself the medication, you could be in pretty bad shape by now."

Ken commended the chief for using the cool cloth on Paul's head. "That cloth really did it, Chief. You brought him out of the delirium so he could at least evaluate his condition and treat himself."

That night Ken and two of his traveling companions slept in the guest hut. Paul stayed in Chief Ndeke's house. Paul dozed on and off, for Nasara's words kept coming back to him. He had just dozed off again when someone near the hut yelled, "Fire!"

Chief Ndeke scrambled out of his bed and grabbed his flashlight. In seconds he was outside and running toward the guesthouse. The flames were already leaping high into the night sky.

"It's the guesthouse!" someone called from back in the village. "Are the men still in there?"

"They're still in there, Chief Ndeke," answered one of the men standing near the building. "I can hear them calling for help. They are trapped."

As the fire roared toward the back of the building, a figure dashed through the flames out the narrow doorway. Seconds later another followed. Both men fell to the ground, their clothing in flames. Several women ran to them and threw water on their burning clothing. Chief Ndeke was beside them immediately.

"Dr. Simms, are you all right?" questioned the concerned leader. "Where is the third man?"

A bank of sparks shot into the night sky as the roof fell in. The thought of his African friend inside the burning building was a crushing blow to Ken. He put his face in his hands as he lay on the ground. The shock seemed unbearable.

"He's gone," Ken whispered to himself. "Beta is gone."

With help from Chief Ndeke, Ken stood to his feet. Nearby was Kada, his clothing still smoldering. His burns were more severe than Ken's and he was in a lot of pain. The missionary doctor felt helpless. All his medicines were destroyed in the fire. Some of the village men helped Ken to the side of his suffering friend. A quick look showed the burns to be on Kada's arms, legs and head. Ken was relieved to see that they were not deep. He asked Chief Ndeke to have the fire victim carried over to his house. He treated Kada's burns along with his own as soon as he could. One of the women in the village had a bottle of palm oil which Ken used to ease the painful burn areas.

The body of Beta was discovered just inside the doorway of the guesthouse. He had tried to follow his two friends through the flames but collapsed before he could get out of the building. In fifteen minutes the charred body was pulled outside and placed in a large grain basket. The villagers were stunned to see such a tragedy and especially to have it happen to men who had come to help them.

Ken suggested that Beta's body be buried immediately and that, as soon as it was daylight, a message be sent to Yanga One and Yanga Two informing the Africans and missionaries what had happened. At the first sign of dawn, a messenger was dispatched to the two villages.

"If I only had my medicine bag, Chief Ndeke, I could take care of these burns better. As it is, I don't have any medicine at all," said Ken.

"You have put my mind to working again, Dr. Simms. Just as soon as it is possible to do so, we must have two things here at Good News. The first thing is a permanent meeting place for preaching services and the other is to have a dispensary where you or one of your nurses can come and treat my people. We will build you a house, which will be for those who come to help us. If someone would come permanently, we would build a larger house."

"That's very kind of you, Chief Ndeke." The missionary doctor hesitated and then asked the village leader about Nasara, for Paul had told Ken about Nasara's threat the evening before. Now the chief, looking disturbed, said thoughtfully that the fire had not been an accident and that he was sure someone had set it purposely.

"There are only a few people in my village who would do such a thing," Ndeke said after Ken told him about Nasara. "Nasara is one of them. I've sent for him to come and see me but I'm told he is not in the village."

By evening the word had spread throughout Good News that Nasara had started the fire and had fled into the forests.

As soon as word of the fire reached Yanga One, Chief Paul sent out an urgent message by way of the talking drums requesting that men bring their bicycles to Yanga One immediately. Within thirty minutes ten men had arrived ready for the trip to bring out the fire victims and Paul Davis. A bicyclist sped to Yanga Two with the news of the fire. Dale Banks left immediately for Yanga One where he joined the rescue party.

Paul's first-aid kit was with him in the chief's hut, enabling him to continue his malaria treatment. His recovery was rapid. By the time Dale arrived the next morning, he was pretty much back to normal. How good it was to see their co-worker. That night the three missionaries talked about the tragedy.

"But how do they know Nasara did it?" asked Dale.

"Chief Ndeke says that one of the women saw him," responded Paul. "She came out to get some wood for her fire and saw him light the grass roof. She was afraid to say anything to anyone for fear he would harm her or her children. He ran off into the jungle and no one has seen him all day."

At that very moment, Nasara was lying helpless beside a jungle stream. He had made his way there after having been bitten by a snake—the deadly green mamba.

24
Emergency Ward

One week to the day that he left Yanga Two to help Paul Davis, Ken Simms and the party returned. In order to make the trip to Yanga One possible, Chief Ndeke had his men make stretchers from bamboo poles and blankets. With four men assigned to a stretcher, the group made the trip in good time. The villagers of Yanga One and Yanga Two united for a praise service. They also mourned for Beta's widow. To show his respect and appreciation for what Beta had done for his village, Chief Ndeke had purchased three baskets of manioc, a basket of peanuts and three goats.

Within a few days life had settled down to its normal hectic routine. The Banks returned to the capital; Dr. and Mrs. Simms and Paul continued their ministries at Yanga One and Yanga Two. Often Nasara's name was mentioned.

Three weeks later the news arrived at the two Yangas that Nasara's remains had been found. Two fishermen from Good News had recognized his clothing.

"I'm sorry he's dead," said Paul. "I'm certain he never accepted the Lord. But he threatened the Lord's work and possibly God removed him."

"It is certainly a sad ending," added Ken, "but we know our lives are no longer in jeopardy."

The days passed into weeks and the weeks into months. Marie's letters kept the missionaries informed of the happenings in France. She was nearing the completion of her first year in college and wrote that she liked her studies better with each passing day. "I just can't seem to get enough of school," she wrote. "The Bible is such a thrilling Book to study. I think I could sit and listen to its teachings forever."

The missionaries were a bit surprised when Marie told of a fellow Bible school student who was showing interest in her. "His wife died of cancer two years ago. I've told him about Martin. Having gone through the same sorrowful experience, we seem to understand each other's loneliness."

Marie always seemed to save a choice bit of news for the end of her letters. This particular letter was no exception. "I'm sure you all will rejoice with me when I tell you that Henry Duval is taking Bible correspondence courses. I thank God every day for what He has done in the lives of these dear friends."

By June, one could easily sense the mounting excitement regarding the coming events—Tene's graduation and marriage to Ruth as well as Paul's marriage to Ann Steele. The news of the first Bible school graduate from Yanga One had made its way among the area villages. For the occasion, Chief Paul sent invitations to several hundred people, inviting them to participate in a feast at Yanga One four days after the graduation. This would give those who attended the graduation ceremonies at the Bible school station plenty of time to travel back to Yanga One.

Not only were all the missionaries among those invited but also a number of governmental officials. To help in the transportation, Ken and Paul decided they should take their pickups to the graduation. Chief Paul asked if he, along with John, the former witch doctor, and Chief Ndeke, could ride together. The three men had become close friends.

"I don't see why you can't travel together," said Ken. "I plan to take Pastor and Mrs. Kondo as well as Ruth. Oh, yes, Katcha asked if she could go too, so I'll take her in my truck." The missionary doctor had not been able to resist the pleading look in Katcha's big brown eyes when she asked if she could go to the graduation.

To complete his load of passengers, Ken took several of the women from the workmen's village at Yanga Two. He built several benches and placed them in the back of the truck.

Paul completed his load by taking a number of station workmen from Yanga Two. Since Ken had the women in his truck, it was decided that he would take the lead. In case of any trouble on the road, the men would be following a short distance behind.

The travelers all gathered for prayer underneath the large flamboyant tree beside the driveway. Someone started to sing as the two trucks started up the long drive to the main road.

> We have heard the joyful sound:
> Jesus saves! Jesus saves!
> Spread the tidings all around:
> Jesus saves! Jesus saves!

"God has done many wonderful things among us, Mr. Davis," said Chief Paul, leaning forward to look past Chief Ndeke, who was seated in the center. "And to think that tomorrow I will see my son graduating from Bible school. My people at Yanga Two love that boy. He and Ruth will make a fine couple."

Paul thought he heard a slight catch in Chief Paul's voice as he spoke. The veteran chief always spoke with authority, but his close friends knew that he had a very soft heart. At times it came through, even though he tried his best to hide it.

"I rejoice with you, Chief Paul," responded Paul. "I know this means a lot to you personally. God has used you from the very beginning of the battle for Yanga."

"And a battle it has been, Mr. Davis," said the chief, smiling. "I really shudder to think what it would be today if Tene had hit you or . . . or . . . Mrs. Davis."

Chief Paul's voice trailed off as he spoke of Becky Davis. The Africans had made it a rule among themselves not to talk about her unless the missionaries brought up the subject first.

"All I can say, Chief Paul, is that the Lord directed that spear. He had another way to call Mrs. Davis to Heaven; and as for me, He had more work for me to do."

Paul kept the pickup just far enough behind Ken's truck to allow the dust to settle. Now and then they would get close enough to see someone wave from the leading truck.

"Can you see Paul's truck?" Marge asked Ken as they neared the end of a long, level stretch across a wide plain.

"I can see a cloud of dust but that's all," answered Ken, glancing in his side-view mirror. "He must be about a mile back."

Every now and then one of the women would laugh and call out, "There they are!" or, "I see them!"

An hour had gone by without any indication from the women that they had seen the truck. Pastor Kondo, the only man in the back of the Simms truck, was unusually quiet. He kept his eyes glued to the road behind them. Hesitantly he reached his arm over the top of the cab and tapped hard enough for Ken to hear him. Immediately the pickup came to a stop. The curious doctor stepped out.

"What is it, Pastor Kondo? Is something wrong?"

"I'm . . . I'm not sure. Dr. Simms. I've been looking for Mr. Davis's truck for the past hour and haven't seen any sign of it. Maybe he has had trouble."

Immediately Ken was on his way back. The Africans sat in silence as they thought of their friends and what may have happened to them. The road with its ruts and stones made the progress slow at times. Nearly an hour passed before they spotted the truck and its occupants. The blue pickup was lying on its side over a small embankment. Several people were stretched out on the ground underneath a tree. Ken brought the truck to a stop and ran to Paul, who was sitting with a bandage around his head.

"Are any of you seriously hurt, Paul?" called the doctor, kneeling down by his co-worker.

"I . . . I . . . think so," stammered Paul in a daze. "Take a look at Chief Paul. He's over there. I've done what I can for him. He may be gone."

Ken felt a weak pulse as he held the chief's wrist. "He's lost a lot of blood. Those cuts on his arm are bad. He may have some internal injuries, too."

Chief Ndeke sat nearby with his head in his hands. He had a large bump above his right eye. The leader from Good News insisted, however, that he was all right and that Ken should care for the more serious cases.

Marge asked Pastor Kondo to take Ken's medical bag to him and surveyed the victims to see who needed help the most.

"It's a miracle no one was killed when the truck turned over," spoke the young wife. "I don't see any broken bones, Ken. Some of them do need sutures."

"Probably all of them in the back of the truck were thrown clear," responded Ken, looking over a list of possible blood donors in a small book he carried in his medicine satchel. "Well, what do you know? I'm the only one on my list who can give blood to Chief Paul," spoke Ken. He asked Marge to get things ready for the transfusion. "I'm afraid Chief Paul won't make it if we don't replace some of the blood he has lost."

"Can I help, Ken?" asked Paul, starting to get to his feet.

Before Ken could answer, Paul collapsed to the ground. Ken rushed to his side. "Bring me some blankets from the box in the truck, Kondo! Mr. Davis is more seriously injured than I first thought."

Under Marge's capable leadership, the scene of the accident soon took on the look of an emergency ward. The box in the back of the pickup yielded blankets, drinking water and even a small amount of medical equipment and medicines. In minutes Paul was conscious and thankful for the warm blankets.

"I'm sorry I can't be of any help, Ken. I guess I must have fainted."

"You'll be all right in a little while, Paul. Just as soon as I give this blood to Chief Paul, I'll be back with you. In the meantime, drink the hot cup of tea Marge has for you and take those two pills. They'll make you feel better."

For the next two hours the doctor and his nurse-wife were busy. The blood transfusion was doing a miracle for the injured chief. Paul was found to have some sore ribs plus a bump on his head, but he was recovering from the light shock he had suffered. Ken, with Marge's assistance, had cared for most of the victims' cuts. Two of the station workmen had badly sprained ankles which were tightly bound with elastic bandages.

Marge directed those who were not hurt in various responsibilities of caring for the injured. Ken had just sat down on a folding chair to drink a cup of coffee when one of the women cried out.

"He's gone, Dr. Simms! Chief Paul is dead!"

Ken jumped to his feet and ran to where his African friend lay on a blanket. A blank expression was fixed on the chief's face.

25
Marie's Decision

It had been a good day for Marie Blanc. She had just completed her first year of Bible college, and to her surprise had done very well. Dr. deCharles paid a special compliment to her on her good accomplishments.

"You had a wonderful year, Marie. I know it was very difficult for you at times, but I want you to know that Mrs. deCharles and I have been praying for you and will continue to do so."

The tall professor halted a moment and then continued. "I trust you won't mind my mentioning this, Marie, but it seems that the relationship between you and Pierre has become rather serious. Am I correct?"

Marie could feel her face getting warm. Not that she was embarrassed about her relationship with Pierre, but the sudden inquiry by the school director surprised her.

"You are correct, Dr. deCharles," responded the young widow. "I know it's been only about a year since Martin went Home to be with the Lord, but I believe He has brought Pierre into my life. We love each other, Dr. deCharles, and Pierre has asked me to marry him."

Marie thought her words might bring a mild rebuke from the director but instead he looked at her and smiled.

"This news does not surprise me, Marie. In fact, I would have been disappointed had you not told me about it. When is the wedding?"

The positive reaction of Dr. deCharles was a great encouragement to Marie. The young widow found it easier to tell him of their tentative plans. "We were going to come tomorrow and talk with you. You see, sir, with your permission, we would like to be married before school begins in September. Pierre has suggested September first as the date."

"I think that's great, Marie. I see no reason why you two should not get married. You both already have the advantage of knowing the responsibility of married life. Yes, you have my permission."

The happy student shook the professor's hand and thanked him for his encouraging words. "I must hurry home, Dr. deCharles. I have some very important letters to write tonight."

Pierre usually met with Marie after class, but his new job demanded nearly all the hours right after school. He knew he needed to earn as much as possible for his forthcoming marriage.

On her way home, Marie became troubled as she thought of her love for Pierre and her own commitment to go to Africa as a missionary. She had often spoken with Pierre concerning missions and always found him open to the Lord's leading regarding the matter. He had said that he would go to Africa, but she wished he would be more specific and positive. Maybe this was a side of Pierre that she did not quite know. Perhaps he was the kind of person who made such decisions without any noticeable fanfare on his part. One thing was certain, Marie knew that she would have to talk with him more on the subject before their marriage took place.

Arriving home, Marie found two letters in her mailbox. One was from Ken and Marge Simms and the other was from Ann Steele. Over the past months, Marie and Ann had developed a good relationship by correspondence. It was decided between them that they both write in English since Marie's grasp of English was better than Ann's knowledge of French.

"We are getting ready for the big weddings which will soon take place here at Yanga Two," wrote Marge. "We are all very anxious to see Ann again. She was such a great blessing to us and the Africans really love her."

Ann's letter also referred to her marriage to Paul Davis. "Just one month and I will be going to the mission's Candidate Seminar. I plan to have my suitcases packed so I can leave after Seminar. My shots are nearly completed for which I'm thankful."

The next part of Ann's letter was especially interesting to Marie. "I'm sure you, too, must be very excited as you prepare for a nursing ministry in Africa. I've tried to imagine what it will be like to be there with you and the missionaries who are already there. God has given me such wonderful peace about it all. How I thank Him for all that He has done in bringing Paul into my life and for the way He has directed me to serve Him in that needy land."

Marie thought over Ann's words. Slowly she repeated them. "God has given me such wonderful peace about it all."

"Dear Lord," prayed Marie, "please give me that same peace. I want to do Your will no matter what it is." The young widow remained with her head bowed, searching the depths of her heart. "Perhaps You've changed the direction for my life, Lord. If it's not Africa, that is perfectly all right with me. I only desire Your will."

Since Pierre had to work late, he and Marie had decided not to see each other that evening. She could now see that it was a wise decision. She wanted to spend more time in prayer concerning her future ministry and how it related to Pierre. As the evening passed, Marie Blanc did receive the peace she prayed for. Rather than what she had expected, she became more certain that she was not to go to Africa. That night as she lay on her bed, she thought of the events of the evening and she felt good inside. "I don't understand it all, Father, but I know You have spoken to me tonight. Thank You, dear Lord, for Your faithfulness."

Marie slept soundly throughout the night. When she awakened the next morning, she was certain Africa was not in the picture for her. She must tell Pierre as soon as possible. Then, too, there were letters to write to Ann Steele and her missionary friends.

Marie had just sat down to eat her breakfast when the phone rang. Wondering who would be calling so early in the morning, Marie picked up the receiver.

"Hello," she said in her cheerful voice.

"Hello, Marie. How are you this morning?"

"I'm fine, thank you, Pierre. And what is your excuse for calling me so early in the day?" Marie teased.

"Marie, I have to go to work early today. One of the men is sick and the boss asked me if I would cover for him. It's overtime pay and I can use the money."

Marie sensed a reserve in Pierre's voice. "Is something wrong, Pierre?"

"I guess you know me better than I thought. Since you ask, there is something that has been on my heart. In fact, I slept very little last night thinking about it. I wanted to speak with you face-to-face; but now with my boss calling, that is not possible."

"What is it, Pierre?" asked Marie softly.

"First of all, I want you to know I love you." The young man's voice trembled as he spoke. "What I am about to tell you in no way reflects a lessening of my love for you." There was silence as Pierre regained his composure.

"More than anything else in the world, Marie, I want the Lord's will in your life. I was certain in my own heart that God brought you into my life, but I must confess to you that I have really never had a missionary call to Africa. I guess what I'm saying, Marie, is that perhaps the best thing for us is not to see each other any more."

The tears welled up in Marie's eyes as she listened to Pierre share his thoughts with her. He, too, wanted God's will for both their lives, even if it meant not marrying Marie.

"I love you, Pierre," said Marie. "Your words come as an answer to prayer."

"What do you mean, Marie?"

"Well, last night I read a letter from Ann Steele, telling me of the wonderful peace she had experienced about being a missionary in Africa. I knew I did not possess that kind of peace. I spent time with the Lord, willing to accept whatever He had for me. I knew my heart was open before Him. It was then that the Spirit of God gave me perfect peace about not going to Africa. As I told the Lord, Pierre, I don't understand His way of doing some things, but I certainly accept it."

"I don't know what to say," Pierre spoke quietly.

"If you hadn't called me, Pierre, I was going to call you. I just had to tell you that our engagement was over because I didn't want to stand in your way of going to Africa."

"You mean to say we both were going to call off our marriage because we did not want to interfere with the other being a missionary in Africa?" The trembling in Pierre's voice disappeared as the picture changed before him.

"That's right, Pierre," responded Marie. "Now, who would ever have thought it would turn out like this in our telephone conversation this morning?"

"The Lord knew all about it," said Pierre. "By the way, will you still be my wife?" Laughter followed spontaneously.

"Listen to what Dr. deCharles told me yesterday, Pierre. He said that he saw no reason why we shouldn't get married." The happy couple talked for another ten minutes while Marie shared the details of her conversation with the professor.

Marie felt a burden had lifted as she hung up the receiver. Picking up her box of stationery, she went out on the front veranda to sit on the swing. Once settled in her favorite writing spot, she began the first letter to Ken and Marge Simms. She felt her missionary friends should be the first to know of her decisions; first, she would not be coming to Africa and second, she would be marrying Pierre before the start of the fall semester.

Marie was certain that her missionary friends would understand her decision. She wondered, however, how the Africans would receive the news that Martin Blanc's widow would not be coming to live and work among them.

26

Two Letters

Kneeling beside the still body of Chief Paul, Ken Simms feared the worst. Gently, he took the chief's wrist. The little group watched in silence as the doctor felt for his pulse.

"He's alive!" called Ken to Paul, whose face revealed great concern. "Chief Paul is alive!" Ken's voice brought a trace of a smile to Chief Paul's face. Slowly his eyes opened and he looked up at his friend.

"Of... of... course, I'm alive," stammered the chief weakly. "I... I... think I fell asleep, Dr. Simms. It must be that medicine you gave me."

"You were sleeping, Chief Paul. I'm sorry I woke you up. You can...."

The sound of a truck motor brought Ken's conversation to a halt. Coming around a curve a quarter of a mile away was the administrator's truck from the post near Yanga Two. The dark green Renault came to a stop and the chauffeur, along with several soldiers, ran to the scene of the accident.

"Hello, Dr. Simms," called the chauffeur. "What has happened? Is anyone badly hurt?"

"I think we have everything under control," answered Ken. "I would like your men to help me get Mr. Davis's truck back on its wheels and if you have any extra oil and gasoline, I would like to buy some from you."

"I have both, Dr. Simms," replied the chauffeur. "The administrator always insists that I carry a good reserve of both. In fact, I'm on my way to the capital to get supplies for him. I can replace anything I sell to you."

In fifteen minutes, Paul's truck was sitting upright. Surprisingly, it had only a few dents in the fenders and door. There was also a broken window. Some of the soldiers crawled under the front of the truck and with the help of the administrator's personal mechanic, soon had the tie-rod back together. To reinforce the tie-rod ends, strips of inner tube were tied tightly around them.

"I'll give you my word that that won't happen again as long as those straps are there," said the mechanic smiling. "Those things hold like iron. But, then, they have to be strong. The roads sure are rough on these trucks."

"I'll say they are," answered Ken. "We had this same thing happen not too long ago with Mr. Banks's car when he came to see us. In fact, it happened near here."

Within an hour, Paul's truck was back on the road and ready to run. Ken decided he would drive the damaged truck and Marge would drive theirs. A suspended stretcher was fixed up in the back of the Simms's truck, with inner tube straps tied to the corners of the four-foot high rack which ran around the sides of the bed of the truck. This would take the roughness out of the ride for Chief Paul. Chief Ndeke and John rode in the truck with Chief Paul. Paul rode in the cab of his truck with Ken.

"I never saw the rut," explained Paul as he described what had happened. "I was traveling just far enough behind you to keep out of your dust. I know most of the bad places in the road, but before I realized what was happening, the truck was out of control and went over that little bank, turning over as it went."

"Praise the Lord, the people either jumped or were thrown clear of the truck when it rolled over," added Ken.

The two friends talked until Paul felt he needed to rest. As best he could, he curled up on the seat of the cab beside Ken. By the time the three trucks arrived at the Bible school station, it was dark. Bill and Kathy Dykes were just about to leave in search of their friends. Like clockwork, the injured were placed on camp cots in two of the guest bedrooms. Chief Paul had made the trip well, but showed signs of fatigue. Ken made a check of the injured before he and Marge retired for the night. Several bandages had to be changed, but he was satisfied with their general condition.

"I don't think any of the injured will have to go to the hospital at the capital," Ken said to Marge after he made the rounds.

"Not even Chief Paul?" asked Marge.

"No, not even the chief," said Ken. "The transfusion did him a lot of good. He's responding better than I thought he would."

"What about Paul?" Marge asked, "He still seems a bit dazed."

"I think he'll feel a lot better by morning. It was a shock to him to have this happen. The injuries to the Africans hit him hard."

Ken's words proved true. By morning there was good improvement in every case. Chief Paul wanted to get up with the others, but Ken persuaded him to stay down until afternoon.

Plans for the graduation were going along as scheduled, and by evening over a thousand people gathered for the special event. Tene's attention was divided in several directions. Ruth, his bride-to-be, was present for the occasion. Chief Paul, his adopted father, had been injured in an accident on the way to his graduation. Many of his close friends, including the missionaries, had come to see him and his classmates graduate. Then, too, there had been the practice session in the afternoon for the evening service. It was a full, busy day for Tene, and by evening he, too, was showing signs of fatigue.

The missionaries arranged for Chief Paul to sit in a soft-cushioned chaise lounge for the service. In spite of his near fatal accident, the village leader showed few signs of any physical problems.

The service was carried out beautifully. Chief Paul was asked to close with prayer. As is typical with most Africans, he recounted in his prayer the happenings of the spiritual battle for Yanga One. He mentioned how the one who nearly took the life of the missionary with his spear was now among those graduating. He spoke of his mother, Bio, and her vital involvement. He praised the Lord for saving Martin and Marie Blanc. Coming to the end of his prayer, he prayed for the two weddings soon to take place and thanked God for sparing their lives in the accident the day before. He then asked God to bless the feast which would be held at Yanga One in a few days. After twenty-five minutes, he ended his prayer. There was a loud chorus of "amens" throughout the auditorium.

"That was a good prayer," Pastor Kondo whispered to Bill Dykes. "Our people like long prayers when there is some meat in them." The veteran missionary knew what the pastor meant. He had often been in prayer meetings that lasted two and three hours.

It took nearly two hours for the people to leave the church. Many had not seen each other for years. The students lined up in front of the auditorium to receive best wishes from their friends. By the time everyone got back to the mission house, it was midnight. Excitement was running high and Ken finally had to tell the injured that they had had enough for one day. An hour later the house was filled with the sound of snoring. Chief Paul must have been the most contented, thought Ken, since his snores could be heard above the others.

More work was done on Paul's pickup to prepare it for the trip back to Yanga Two. Bill Dykes had a heavy sheet of clear plexiglass which was cut to serve as a window. When installed, it worked perfectly. New tie-rods were found in Bill's supply of parts and put on the truck. To help each other in case of truck problems, Bill, Ken and Paul had purchased the same model truck. Between them they usually had a needed part.

Because of the number of injured, it was decided to stay over one more day. This extra time would also allow more work to be done on Paul's truck. The decision was a wise one for all. Just before the two trucks were to leave for Yanga Two, the mail bus from the capital arrived, bringing with it the mail for the up-country posts. Ken was able to get the mission mail at the local post office.

In the week's mail was a letter from Marie. She told of her planned marriage to Pierre and that she felt God had redirected her path away from Africa.

"Please share this news with Chief Paul. I'm sure it would have been exciting to live there among all of you, but the Lord knows best and it is His will that really counts."

In the same mail was a letter to Paul from Ann. He read the letter as he sat on the front veranda of the mission house. "It won't be long now until I appear before the General Council for my doctrinal examination. I'm getting more excited every day. Please tell Chief Paul that I can hardly wait to get there to begin my medical work among his people. I know this is God's will for my life."

Ann then went on to talk about their wedding. Paul had written to tell her that the double ceremony would take place August 10. This would give her about two weeks to get to Yanga Two after the close of Candidate Seminar.

After finishing Ann's letter, Paul went to a nearby shade tree where Chief Paul had asked to be seated in a chaise lounge. "The house is too little for all these friends to crowd inside," he had mentioned to Bill Dykes. "Just let me sit under that big tree out there and I can talk to many of the visitors at the same time."

Paul arrived at the chief's side the same time as Ken. "There is something in Marie's letter which I want you both to hear," said Ken. The leader from Yanga One frowned as he listened to Ken read the letter from France. When the doctor had finished, Chief Paul held up a finger to indicate he wanted to say something.

"Does God lead a person in two directions, Dr. Simms? Did He call her to Africa or didn't He?"

Ken and Paul looked at each other. Ken responded. "We must leave that between Marie and the Lord, Chief Paul. I know that God doesn't play games with our lives. At the same time, I feel certain that Marie knows His will for her life."

Chief Paul nodded, indicating he understood.

Paul then read part of the letter from Ann. Chief Paul's face brightened as he listened. "Even though I know Miss Ann is coming, it gives me much joy every time I hear of her progress. God knew all about Marie's decision beforehand. It's wonderful the way He works things out."

The wise chief looked up at Paul and grinned. Then he added, "and when we get Miss Ann, we get Mr. Davis, too."

The three men laughed, shook hands, and Paul and Ken went back to their task of preparing for the return trip. Again, Ken insisted that Chief Paul travel in the suspended stretcher in the back of one of the trucks. "After all," he told the leader, "we want you in good shape for this welcome home feast for Tene."

Determined to carry out his self-imposed assignment, Chief Ndeke took the place nearest the stretcher. This would give him further opportunity to discuss matters of establishing an outpost in his village with Chief Paul. His visit to the Bible school fueled the flame in his heart to begin a spiritual work at Good News.

27

Tene's Spear Returns

The news of the accident had reached every village between the Bible school village and Yanga One. When the villagers saw the two pickups approaching, they shouted greetings to the travelers. Chief Paul, lying in the stretcher, waved with both arms. He wore a continuous grin on his face.

"He's having a great time back there," said Marge as they passed through a village.

"That's good medicine for him," replied Ken. "He has improved greatly the past two days."

The reception at Yanga Two was tremendous. The people in the workmen's village fixed huge arches of palm leaves and bougainvilleas every 150 feet over the long driveway. The people pressed hard against the trucks, trying to shake the hands of their returned friends. Many had picked bouquets of wild flowers to give to them as well. Chief Paul seemed to be the center of attention. The African grapevine brought a detailed account of all that had happened in the accident.

Knowing that Chief Paul was anxious to get home, Pastor Kondo immediately saw to it that all passengers for Yanga One were transferred to Ken's truck. In about thirty minutes, the blue pickup headed back up the driveway on its way to the miracle village. The closer they got to home, the more excited the group became. Someone began to sing and in seconds all joined in. The people at Yanga One heard the singing even before they could see the truck.

"We're home!" shouted the happy passengers as Ken pulled into the village. Over five hundred people gathered to welcome Tene and Chief Paul home. Chief Paul and Chief Ndeke were asked to sit on either side of Tene in the middle of the village. The people at Yanga One then proceeded to carry out a planned program of songs and testimonies. The children sang a song especially dedicated to Tene, "I Will Make You Fishers of Men." Ken smiled as he noticed that nearly everyone in the crowd tried to do the motions with the children.

"That's a good one, children," called Chief Paul. "Do that one over again but go slower this time so Chief Ndeke and I can do those motions."

As soon as the singing was finished, Ken shook hands with the two chiefs and Tene and headed back to Yanga Two. He warned his patient not to try to do too much. As he drove he prayed, "Thank You, Father, for sparing everyone's lives in the accident. Thank You, too, that Chief Paul has regained his strength so quickly. Lord, continue to guide Marie. I believe she is in Your will. Help the people at Yanga One to understand."

The time passed quickly and Ken was back home before he realized it. Some of the crowd that had gathered to welcome the travelers home were still there when Ken arrived. Everyone was in a festive mood.

"After all," Marge said that evening, "who would turn down a free meal? Chief Paul may not realize it, but he's going to have at least two thousand people at his feast for Tene."

"And I'm not going to eat until then," chimed in Paul. "I told Chief Paul I was going to take advantage of his invitation."

The smile disappeared from Paul's face and was replaced with a grimace. In a mock-serious tone he continued, "I'll take advantage of his invitation only if he leaves out his speciality—manioc and caterpillar sauce." The three friends burst into laughter. How could they ever forget the joke that their African friend had played on them?

The following day the area people began to converge on Yanga One. Sensing it would be a larger crowd than he had expected, Chief Paul sent out for extra food. Surrounding the entire village of Yanga One were small temporary businesses—set up overnight.

Tailors took advantage of the large crowd by displaying their wares. Beautifully colored cloth hung from several of the grass mat shelters. Kerosene lamps, cans of sardines, soap, nails, rock salt, cubed sugar, tin cups and plastic sandals could be found almost everywhere. One store clerk even brought several bicycles which he put on display.

That evening approximately two thousand people crammed into the village of Yanga One. People were everywhere. Chief Paul sent a messenger asking the Simmses and Paul Davis to come that night. Upon their arrival he took them into his hut.

"I never thought we would have this many people. I've sent out for more food so I don't think there will be a problem in feeding them."

The chief picked up his Bible. "My village has never seen so many people before. Dr. Simms and Mr. Davis, I'm asking you two men to plan a way in which everyone will hear the gospel tomorrow. Can you do that for me?"

Paul looked at Ken. "I happen to have my amplifying system with me, Ken. I'm sure that's loud enough for everyone to hear. I brought the three speakers, too."

"That's good," commented Chief Paul. "Before they eat tomorrow morning, they will hear the gospel. Then, before they go home tomorrow afternoon, they will hear it again. Will you men speak?"

"I think we all should say something, Chief Paul," answered Paul. "After all, what greater testimonies are there to hear than those from you and Tene?"

That night, in spite of the excitement in the village, Chief Paul spent time in prayer. He knew there were hundreds of unsaved people in his village, and it caused him inward pain to think of any of them going back to their homes not knowing Jesus.

Ken, Marge and Paul stayed in two of the rooms in the new dispensary building. Most of the people slept on grass mats wherever they could find a place to stretch one out. The talking among the people finally gave way to whispering and then slowly to snoring. By two in the morning, the village of Yanga One was asleep. Paul finally had to close his window to keep out the noise of all the snoring.

The gray dawn brought a stirring among the many visitors. Chief Paul was out early making sure everyone was comfortable and enjoying the occasion. Tene had already told his story of conversion and Bible school experience many times. By eight o'clock, the people sat in small groups throughout the village. A number of women had worked most of the night preparing the food at one end of the village. The sour smell of manioc blended with the aroma of coffee drifted through the town. As soon as the loudspeakers were in place, Chief Paul spoke to the people.

"My friends, today is a special day for the village of Yanga One. Our own Tene has graduated from Bible school and has come back home to work for God among us. I have asked Dr. Simms and Mr. Davis to take charge of this service. Whatever they do or say is all right with me."

"Hello, friends," came the voice of Ken Simms. "First of all, I want to publicly thank God for sparing the lives of our friends in their recent accident." A loud clicking of tongues could be heard throughout the crowd. "Chief Paul is still weak in body and Mr. Davis has not yet fully regained his strength. There are others among you who show wounds of the accident. But God spared their lives and they are with us today."

"A few years ago, Tene had an experience of throwing a spear." The crowd sensed Ken's amusing remark and began to snicker. "In fact, he just about gave my co-worker, Mr. Davis, a haircut."

The crowd erupted with laughter and handclapping. Tene looked at Paul and the two patted each other on the shoulder.

"Today, those two men are brothers in Christ. I've asked Tene to share with you his testimony of what God has done in his life."

The recent Bible school graduate walked to the mike, which was located under a tree. Nervously, he cleared his throat and began to speak. "Greetings, my friends." The sound of hums came from the crowd as they responded to Tene's greeting. "It would take me all day to give you an account of my life since God saved me, so, I will tell you how I got saved and how God led me to Bible school."

For the next half hour, Tene told of some of his past. He acted out how he threw the spear through the window of the mission house at Yanga Two, narrowly missing Paul and Becky Davis. Unknown to Tene, Paul had brought the spear with him to the feast. As Tene continued to describe the details of that night, Paul came out from behind a nearby hut, carrying the spear.

"That's my spear," called Tene, surprised to see it again. "Where did you get it, Mr. Davis? That happened so long ago."

"It's been right there in the mission house, Tene," answered Paul. "It serves to remind me of several things—God's protecting hand and His love and grace toward you. Today we play with it, but that night it was meant to kill."

Tene took the spear from his friend and held it high. "This, my friends, is a perfect example of what Jesus can do in a person's life. I didn't know the true God back then. I worshiped bones and animals and gods made with my hands. You know what I'm talking about, because many of you sitting here today worship those things now."

Many of the people nodded their heads, agreeing with Tene. Others showed their approval by clicking their tongues. Chief Paul's face was a picture of contentment as he listened to his adopted son.

"You have come at the invitation of my father, Chief Paul, to help us celebrate my graduation. I'm glad you came and I thank you. However, if you return home without Jesus as your Savior, you leave us with hearts burdened for you. We want you to know Jesus. He is ready to forgive you of your sinful ways, of your religious practices. Won't you do as I did one day and accept Him into your heart? It doesn't cost any money and you can't work for it. Jesus has already paid the price for your sins. You can have your sins forgiven and receive eternal life right now, right where you are."

When Tene finished speaking, two thousand people sat in complete silence. Several were wiping the tears from their eyes.

"What do we do now?" Tene asked Ken.

"We're going to give an invitation," answered the doctor.

"God is working in hearts, Dr. Simms," added Chief Paul. "I think you are wise in giving an invitation now."

During the next fifteen minutes, over one hundred men and women responded to the invitation to receive Christ. Paul Davis directed some of the more mature Christians from Yanga One and Yanga Two to talk with those making decisions. Chief Paul was thrilled when he saw some of his old friends among the one hundred.

"I had a message to preach this morning, Chief Paul," said Ken, "but I'm not going to give it now. Tene said it all. The gospel just can't be given any clearer than what we heard today from that young man."

"You're in charge, Dr. Simms," the African leader responded. "Whatever you do is all right with me."

By eleven o'clock the women were passing out the food. The people divided into small groups of five to seven. In the center of each group was placed a large bowl of hot steaming manioc along with a bowl of meat chunks and gravy. Steaming hot glasses of coffee were served to each one along with a good supply of sugar cubes. Prayer was offered to the Lord for the food by Chief Paul and the signal to begin eating was given.

The smacking of lips and the belching sounds could be heard everywhere. Chief Paul smiled as he looked out among the people. "They're happy and they like the food, Mr. Davis. When they belch, that's a good sign."

He took the mike in his hands. "There is plenty of food, my friends. I don't want anyone to go away from Yanga One hungry. At one o'clock we are going to sing some hymns and then Dr. Simms or Mr. Davis will preach to us from God's Word. After that, the feast is over and you can do as you wish."

Several clapped their hands to show their appreciation for the feast. Chief Paul felt good. God had blessed his village with a part-time dispensary work, a pre-Bible school and, now, a full-time pastor. Another reason for rejoicing was the presence of Chief Ndeke and John, the former witch doctor. The village leader knew that great blessings were in store for the area. He realized, too, that Satan was alive and powerful and was not about to give up that territory without a battle.

28

Calling Dr. Simms

The feast day celebration for Tene was the topic of conversation for weeks to follow. Everywhere the missionaries went people spoke to them about that good day at Yanga One.

The last letter from Ann was written the day before she was to leave for the mission's July conference. "I'm really excited to have this opportunity to meet with the General Council. My contacts thus far with the home office staff have been great."

Paul held the letter in his hand as he spoke to Ken and Marge. "Just think, she has already met the council and has nearly completed her Candidate Seminar."

"Go ahead, Paul," teased Marge, "and what else?"

"Well, since you have forced me to say it, we'll be going to the capital in eight days to get her."

In spite of all their teasing, Ken and Marge marveled at the way the Lord had worked in the lives of Paul and Ann. Certainly He had provided the answer to Paul's need.

"I was thrilled to see how Tene has adapted to the work at Yanga One," said Ken as the three missionaries sat on the front veranda drinking iced tea. "When I was there this past Tuesday he had seventy-three children and twenty-one adults in children's class. Chief Paul insists that everyone in the village attends as many classes and church services as possible."

"I think that's wonderful," spoke Marge. "He wants his people to hear the Word of God; and if it's in children's classes that they hear it, that's all right with him."

"It always amazes me how God works things out," Ken added. "We were all counting on Martin and Marie coming to help us. Then Martin died and Marie is marrying Pierre and they aren't even in the picture. Yet everyone seems to be satisfied with Marie's decision."

"That's right, honey," said Marge. "God has helped the people accept the change."

The next week was filled with preparation for the double wedding ceremony as well as the trip to the capital to meet Ann. Paul had received a cablegram informing him that she had successfully passed her oral doctrinal examination before the mission council and would be going on to Candidate Seminar.

Food for the wedding feast was being gathered at Yanga Two when the Simms and Paul left for the capital. Chief Paul wanted to be there when Ann arrived, but he felt that he was needed to supervise the preparations for the weddings as well as the feast which would follow.

Dale and Dorothy Banks had good news for the three up-country missionaries upon their arrival in the capital. A cablegram had arrived from Ann, informing them that she had completed her Candidate Seminar and was now a missionary appointee. Although they had expected this good news, it was still a real joy to hear the finality of it.

"Her deputation is automatically completed and she already has her support," Dale said, kidding with Paul. "You never had it that easy, did you, Dorothy?"

That night the two couples and Paul went to the Palace Restaurant. "This is certainly a lot better than Chief Paul's speciality," said Paul, grinning.

"I don't think I'll ever forget the look on Ken's face," Marge said, laughing.

"He sure disappeared fast enough when he suddenly remembered he was a doctor and had patients to see."

As they were driving home from the restaurant, Marge suddenly became ill. Pains in her abdomen made it almost impossible for her to sit up in the car. At the mission station she was helped into the house. There Ken examined her.

"We'd better take her into the hospital," he told Paul and Dale. "I'm not sure, but I think she may have appendicitis."

In minutes the missionaries were on their way back into the city. "Can we find a surgeon at this time of night?" Paul asked Dale.

"We can call their homes," answered Dale. "If we can't find one of them that way, we can always go look for them."

"I don't think we'll have time for that," added Ken. "This could possibly require immediate surgery."

When they arrived at the hospital, Ken took charge since neither of the French doctors was there.

"I'll call one of them right away, Dr. Simms," called one of the African assistants. "I'm sure I heard Dr. Bouvoir say that he would be home this evening."

Further examination and tests proved Ken's earlier diagnosis to be correct. Surgery was indicated as soon as possible. The attendants prepped Marge while Ken anxiously awaited word from Dr. Bouvoir.

A nurse appeared at the doorway of the scrub room where Ken was getting ready for his possible involvement. "Dr. Bouvoir doesn't answer his phone and Dr. Grandier is out of the city for the night."

Ken faced the inevitable. "I've got to do it," he whispered to himself. "I have to operate on her."

With the decision made for him, the husband-doctor finished scrubbing. He was then fitted with a cap and gown and confidently entered the room. The attendants had already given Marge a spinal. A slight smile appeared on her face when she saw Ken.

"Well, it looks as if yours truly is going to be the cut-up for this one, honey," Ken said, attempting a smile.

"You're the best, Ken," spoke Marge in a low, tired voice. "I'm glad you are the doctor on call tonight."

Bathed in the prayers of his co-workers, Ken took the scalpel, placed it on his wife's body and proceeded to make the incision. The perspiration quickly soaked the front of his cap and the top of his mask. His expertise showed in his every move. Spreading the incision open, he found the infected appendix. Within minutes, it was lying on a tray beside the table.

"I've got it, honey. It's out," he spoke to his half-conscious wife.

"Thank you," responded Marge in a whisper.

Ken had begun closing the incision when the door from the

scrub room opened. In stepped Dr. Bouvoir. "Good evening, Dr. Simms, I'm sorry I couldn't get here sooner." The French doctor was scrubbed and in his gown.

"Good evening, Dr. Bouvoir. I think everything is in order here. Perhaps you can check on this before I close up."

The French surgeon stepped up beside the table and carefully examined the work which Ken had done. "Excellent, Dr. Simms. If you want me to, I can close it up for you."

Ken was relieved to hear Dr. Bouvoir's offer. The hospital staff took over as Ken looked on. Every now and then he would look at Marge and smile.

"It's almost over, honey. Just a few more minutes."

"Finished!" said the Frenchman as he laid the instrument on the tray beside him. "Everything is just fine, Mrs. Simms. It's not every wife who has the opportunity to be operated on by her husband. I must say he did a good job. I don't think I could have been that steady if it had been Mrs. Bouvoir."

Dr. Bouvoir patted Marge on the top of her head as he left the table. "We must have you folks over for dinner before you return up-country." The two men talked a bit in the scrub room and then shook hands.

"Thank you, Dr. Bouvoir, for your help tonight."

"I didn't do much, Dr. Simms. You had the nasty critter out when I got here. Glad I was able to do what I could for you, however."

By the next morning Marge was quite sore, but feeling much better. "I'm going to miss the weddings," she said sadly. The tears began to well up in her eyes."

"Let's not think about that now, honey," comforted Ken. "I'm sure something will be worked out for both couples and it will probably be the best for all."

When the telegrams arrived up-country the next afternoon, Chief Paul, Pastor Kondo and Pastor Tene quickly got together to discuss the latest event.

"The Lord allowed this to happen for a purpose," said Tene. "Ruth and I put off our wedding date two months so we could be married at the same time as Mr. Davis and Miss Ann, and I don't see why we can't reschedule it for a later date."

"Have you talked with Ruth about this?" questioned Chief Paul.

"Just a little bit," responded the young pastor. "I'm sure my future father-in-law won't mind." Tene looked at Pastor Kondo when he spoke.

"I don't mind, Tene, and I know it will be all right with Ruth, too. We love our missionaries and this would be a nice thing to do for them."

"What about the food that has been gathered?" asked Tene.

"No problem with that," Chief Paul answered. "We'll just give what won't keep to the Bible school students and some of the older people in the surrounding villages. I'll tell the chiefs to send men here for it."

"Tene," spoke Chief Paul, "go to the post before it closes and send a telegram for us. Kondo, you put the words in it and Tene will write them down."

By late afternoon a telegram from the two Yangas was placed in the mailbox at the capital for Dale Banks. He would pick it up the next morning on his way to the airport with his wife, Dorothy, and Paul Davis to meet Ann Steele.

29

Questions and Answers

"Thank You, Father, for our dear African Christians. They are so very good to us." After she finished praying, Marge wiped the tears from her eyes. Ann Steele had come to the hospital within an hour of her arrival in the capital, and she and Paul had brought with them the telegram from Chief Paul.

"We don't mind rescheduling our wedding date," said Ann in her sweet voice. "After all, it won't seem right for you not to be there, and the only place for it to be is Yanga Two."

The new arrival kissed Marge on the forehead as she left the hospital room. "They say you'll be coming home tomorrow. I'll just be your slave until you're well enough to travel up-country."

"It's so good to see her again," whispered Marge to herself. "She's so kind. Thank You, Lord, for Ann."

The next morning Ken took Marge back to the mission station. Dorothy had the guest room prepared beautifully. Ann had the second guest room and Paul stayed in a small apartment behind the main mission house. The return to the mission station was a real uplift for Marge. Immediately the teasing came from Dale and Paul.

"Boy, not everyone is escorted home by the doctor," said Paul, winking at Dale.

"And not everyone has free twenty-four-hour personal doctor care either," added Dale. "We had better find out who she is, Paul. She might even be a celebrity."

"All right you fellows," spoke Ann. "Since I'm her nurse, I must order you both out of the room. On your way now." The pretty nurse raised her arms pretending to push them out of the room.

"Come on, Paul," Dale said, pretending to be hurt. "I know when I'm not wanted."

The next day brought a surprise to the mission station. Late in the afternoon the missionaries, including Marge, were sitting on the front veranda. Paul was the first to point out the truck pulling into the driveway from the main road.

"It's a government truck," he said as the vehicle came closer.

"Oh, no! I can't believe my eyes!" Dale called out. "Look who's sitting on the front seat."

"Chief Paul!" exclaimed Paul as he walked to the truck to meet their friend.

"Hello, Mr. Davis. When I heard of Mrs. Simms's illness, I just had to come. Besides, I wanted to see Miss Ann again, too."

The tall chief strode to the veranda and shook hands with his beloved missionaries. When he came to Ann, he bent down and blew gently into her ears.

"Thank you, Chief Paul," said Ann, wiping the tears from her eyes. "It's good to be here . . . and thank you for coming."

The Yanga One leader turned to the government chauffeur and thanked him for the ride. The pleasant-looking driver took off his cap and bowed to the group, then climbed back into the truck. In a minute he was back on the road to the city. Dorothy quietly slipped away from the group and went inside to set another place for their newest guest.

At the evening meal, Chief Paul brought his friends up-to-date on the happenings at Yanga One and Yanga Two. It was decided among them that the wedding date would be September 25, which was about seven weeks away.

"By then you should be feeling well again. If the road is too bumpy, Dr. Simms can put you in one of those beds in the back of the truck held up by rubber straps."

The missionaries laughed with Chief Paul over his remarks to Marge. He seemed to enjoy the foreign missionaries' sense of humor and practiced it on them every chance he had.

Chief Paul and Paul Davis arranged with the government chauffeur from the post near Yanga Two to take them back up-country. It would be nearly a week before he was ready to return. When he arrived to pick them up at the mission station, he insisted that they both sit with him in the cab. Paul was especially happy for the arrangements because the sun and dust made such a long trip uncomfortable. As is usually the case with truck chauffeurs, the driver had managed to pick up seven other passengers.

"Those are paying passengers," Chief Paul whispered to Paul while the chauffeur was outside checking the load in the back of the truck.

"What do you mean by that?" asked Paul.

"He makes them pay just a little less than the bus fare," responded the chief.

"What does he do with the money?" Paul's interest was growing over the men and women sitting up on top of the load.

"He keeps it. They all do it and their bosses know it, but no one does anything about it."

"That explains why I sometimes see people sitting on top of the loads," Paul said with a grin.

"Right!" answered Chief Paul. "In fact, sometimes the load gets top heavy with them and their baggage. Now and then a top-heavy load will cause the truck to tip over. Those bodies up there are shifting their weight as the truck moves."

Paul slowly shook his head. "I see what you mean."

By night the government truck arrived at the post where the Bible school was located. The chauffeur took his two special passengers to the mission station and told them he would pick them up at eight o'clock the next morning.

Bill and Kathy Dykes were glad to see the two men. "Thank you for sending us the telegram about Marge," said Bill. "How is she doing?"

"Oh, she's fine," responded Paul. "That Ken is something else. He had to do practically the entire operation. Dr. Bouvoir felt badly about not being home when they called him from the hospital."

Before they retired for the night, Paul and Chief Paul took a walk over to the Bible school students' village. There they sat with the students around the fire in the center of the village.

"I heard that you have three new students coming to school this next semester, Chief Paul," mentioned one of the men.

"That's correct," answered the chief. "God is doing some wonderful things in the Yanga One area. We plan to have fourteen students in our pre-Bible school classes. Tene, I mean Pastor Tene, is doing well. He is now reaching out into the nearby villages with his classes. Ruth will be a great help to him."

Paul Davis sat listening to the chief and could not help but think of the morning that Ken led Chief Ngonjo to the Lord and how the new Christian took upon himself the name of Paul. Truly the African chief was a perfect example of what God can do in the life of an individual.

The men sang some hymns and then had a time of prayer before Paul and Chief Paul returned to the house. "They're a great group of students," Bill Dykes commented as the chief and Paul entered the house.

"They sure are," reflected Paul. "By the way, you didn't have to wait up for us, did you?"

"Oh, that's all right," answered Bill. "I had some paper work to get done."

The next morning the chauffeur was at the mission station promptly at eight. Paul and the chief thanked their co-workers and were soon on their way. Bill and Kathy watched the heavily loaded truck until it was out of sight.

"What will the administrator say when he sees all those people on his truck?" asked Kathy.

"He won't even see them, honey. I'm sure the chauffeur will have the riders get off right before he enters the post. Paul was telling me Chief Paul's explanation that each one pays to ride up on the load."

The trip to Yanga Two was made without difficulty. No sooner had the truck stopped beside the mission house than the people were asking questions.

"How is Mrs. Simms? Did Miss Ann arrive? When are they coming home? What about the weddings?"

"All right," called out Chief Paul. "Mr. Davis and I will answer your questions but we can only take them one at a time. I will call on you for your questions when I see you raise your hand."

Immediately hands went up all around the crowd. For the next hour, the two men stood and answered questions from their friends. Finally Chief Paul had to call a halt to the question and answer time.

"I have to get on to my village now. When Mr. Davis returns, you can continue with the questions." The chief looked at Paul with a grin. "I'm sure he will know all the answers."

The arrival at Yanga One was similar to that of Yanga Two. The people were filled with questions and the two men stood for forty minutes answering questions before someone suggested that they all have a drink of coffee.

Paul was handed the usual tall glass of strong, black coffee along with a handful of sugar cubes. He always enjoyed watching his African friends put sugar in their coffee. They never stopped with one or two cubes but rather ended up putting ten or more in the glass.

Sitting on the two handmade folding chairs, the men slowly sipped their coffee as they answered more questions. Paul never did allow himself to slurp it long and loud as his African friends did.

After two hours of visiting, Paul decided to return to Yanga Two. As he was about to get into the truck, Chief Paul took him by the arm. "Mr. Davis, my people want me to tell you something."

The look on the chief's face indicated the seriousness of the matter. Paul retraced his steps to where he had been sitting. The villagers looked to their chief for the next words.

"We have a secret, Mr. Davis. We wanted to keep it until Miss Ann arrived; but since the wedding has been set back for about six weeks, my people have decided to let you know what we want to do for you."

The surprised missionary turned to say something and then stopped.

"We will hear you when I'm through telling you our secret, Mr. Davis. I'm sure your words will change by that time," continued Chief Paul. Some of the villagers smiled as their chief spoke.

"As you know, we have needed missionaries here in Yanga One for some time. We thought Martin and Marie were to be those missionaries, but it was not the Lord's will. Now, God has brought you and your wife-to-be, Miss Ann, into the picture. To show our appreciation for wanting to come and live among us, we are going to give you, through official government papers, a piece of land beside our village. It is on the side over there where my mother, Bio, lived."

"I . . . I . . . don't know what to say, Chief Paul," stammered Paul. "Thank you all very much."

"There's one thing more," added the village leader. "We want to give you an outright gift to help you pay for your house. My men will work for you. I will see that they are paid. Out there in that shed are one hundred sacks of cement. We have been bringing them up from the capital on the administrator's truck so you wouldn't know anything about it."

Paul looked in the direction the chief was pointing. There, hidden among the trees on the edge of the village, was a low grass-roofed building. He had seen it before but never thought to ask about it.

"I'm without words, Chief Paul," said Paul in a choked voice.

The elated chief pointed to still another object. It looked like a pile of dried grass to Paul. "Under that grass is enough sand and gravel to build your house. My people have been carrying it from a nearby stream in the forest."

As best he could, Paul thanked Chief Paul and his people. It was difficult for him to speak as he climbed into the pickup. Waving to the crowd from his cab window, Paul's heart was deeply touched.

"Father," he prayed, traveling back home, "they have so little but yet they have given so much. Thank You, Lord, for the privilege of working for You here among them. Help Ann and me to serve You faithfully."

The truck seemed to leap over the dirt road to Yanga Two. In his mind, Paul Davis was picturing a beautiful bride. Ann Steele was in Africa to marry him.

30
Unwelcomed Visitor

Marge Simms made an excellent recovery. Ken kept Paul informed by telegram and letters. The days blended into weeks, and soon it was time for the Simmses and Ann to begin their return trip up-country. Dale and Dorothy decided to follow them in their car.

The missionaries left early in the morning since it was necessary to drive more slowly than usual over the bumpy road. Late in the afternoon, they arrived at the Bible school station where Bill and Kathy had been expecting them.

"You look great," called Kathy as she approached the truck. Marge was sitting on large soft cushions to help take up the shock of the rough road.

"Thank you, Kathy," Marge answered. "I must confess, I'm absolutely spoiled." She pointed to the Banks's car just pulling into the drive. "That Ann is a wonderful nurse. We are fortunate to have such a talented girl in the work here."

Kathy had a lovely meal prepared for the hungry travelers. Ann commented on her homemade bread. "I sure missed this good bread you bake, Kathy."

Before Kathy could answer, Bill teasingly chimed in, "is that all you missed, Ann?"

"Ann's face reddened. "No, I missed a lot of things, and . . . and people." They all laughed at Ann's answer.

After dinner the missionaries, joined by a number of students, sat on the front veranda and talked. Ann, especially, was blessed by the fellowship. One of the things she had missed most was the fellowship with the African believers. Before they retired for the night, one of the students prayed, thanking God for Marge's recovery as well as for the safe arrival of Ann.

"Lord," he prayed, "she's only half here because the other half is at Yanga Two waiting for her. Now when these two halves begin working for You as one, I know that great things will be accomplished. Thank You, Father, for bringing Miss Ann to us."

The next morning, Bill and Kathy joined their co-workers going to Yanga Two. The three vehicles moved at a reduced speed for Marge's benefit as well as to keep together. They stopped under a large shade tree at noon for their picnic lunch.

"This is another thing I missed, Bill," said Ann, grinning as she munched on a sandwich. They all knew that Ann was referring to Bill's comment the night before.

By the time the group got to Yanga Two, the sun was low in the western sky. "I love these African sunsets," Marge told Ken as she gazed off in the distance. "Africa is really beautiful . . . and the people are beautiful, too."

"They really are, honey," Ken answered. "They really are."

Even though darkness was rapidly descending, the little mission station was humming with excitement. Pastor Kondo was the first to shake Marge's hand and to welcome her home. Ann was surrounded by her African friends.

"Have you forgotten our language?" called one elderly woman who bent over and blew gently into Ann's ears.

"No, I can hear you," responded Ann. "I know what you are saying." One of the things that impressed the missionaries was the way Ann had learned to converse in the tribal language.

The gifts for both Marge and Ann were pouring in. Several of the station workmen carried them to the front veranda. Marge counted eleven chickens and three goats among her gifts of peanuts, squash, manioc, sweet potatoes, okra, corn and rice.

After several hundred handshakes and greetings, the missionaries went into the house. Paul and Ann lingered on the veranda as they looked over the gifts.

"What are we going to do with those goats?" Ann asked, looking a bit bewildered.

"Well, we can keep them to raise more goats or we can eat

them. Anything else would be wrong in the African's eyes."

"Eat those poor creatures?" Ann said with a frown on her face. "I could never do that."

"You've done it many times when you were here before," answered Paul, patting one of the goats on the head. "Why, this one here would be good eating."

"Paul Davis!" exclaimed Ann. "I didn't know you were so cruel." Ann knew that goat meat was a specialty among the Africans and it presented no problem to her to eat it. For the sake of teasing Paul, however, she pretended to be offended.

Because of the overflow of guests, Paul decided to sleep out in the garage on a camp cot. "But what about the snakes and lizards?" asked Marge, looking a bit concerned.

"No problem," responded Paul. "I'll just string up a couple of wires and hang my mosquito net on them. That will keep out any little animals."

Ann squeezed Paul's hand as she accompanied him to the door. "Is it safe out there in the garage?" she asked in a whisper.

"Perfectly safe, honey," Paul answered. "Nothing can touch me inside the net, unless . . . unless . . . it's a lion or leopard."

Ann looked nervous. "But they say there are lions and leopards that come into the yard at night."

"I'll close the garage doors, Ann. Besides, once the animal saw who it had, I'm sure it would drop me right away."

Ann watched Paul until he reached the garage. He pulled the large door open and stepped inside, closing it behind him.

The missionaries in the house talked a bit longer and then decided to retire. "Here's a glass for you, Ann," called Marge. "Help yourself to a bottle of water from the fridge."

Ann found that she had to remind herself occasionally that she was not to drink the water directly from the faucet. The water system was simply four 55-gallon barrels erected high alongside the house. From these the water was gravity-fed in pipes throughout the house. Now and then a lizard or mouse would fall into the water and drown. After several days the water would take on a strange smell. That was one of the many reasons for all drinking water to be boiled for thirty minutes and then run through chalky filters. It was then placed in bottles in the kerosene-powered refrigerator.

Whenever anyone brushed his teeth, he would take a bottle of water from the fridge. More than once Ann had caught herself about to brush her teeth with the unboiled water in the faucet.

Pastor Kondo took the goats and chickens given as gifts and put them in a small chicken house at the back of the station. Afterwards, he and Paul sat by a fire near the garage until midnight.

"It's good to have Miss Ann back," said Kondo, scratching a mosquito bite on his ankle.

"It sure is, Kondo," Paul answered. The veteran missionary gazed at the house where he and Becky had once lived. "You know, Kondo, when Mrs. Davis went Home to be with the Lord, I never thought it would be possible for me to love anyone else as I loved her."

The two men sat in silence as Paul paused between sentences. "But there in that house tonight is a woman I love very much. She was brought into my life by the Lord, and that is why it is all so wonderful. The Lord did it, Kondo."

The African pastor reached out to shake Paul's hand. "I thank the Lord for all He has done for you, Mr. Davis. He has kept you here among the people you love and He has provided you another mate who fits into the work like Mrs. Davis did."

The two men had prayer together and then Pastor Kondo made his way back to the workmen's village. As he walked along in the dark, his heart was praising the Lord. He was a very happy man, for his only daughter, Ruth, would soon be a pastor's wife.

Kondo had nearly reached the edge of the village when he noticed a large black object about fifteen feet ahead on the side of the path. He stopped and stood perfectly still. He thought he saw it move. Kondo's heart was pounding hard. A chill rippled through his body. Again he thought it moved. Yes, it did move; he could now see its head. It was a large leopard in a crouched position!

The African pastor had seen many victims of encounters with leopards. Some had their scalps torn nearly off. Others had eyes destroyed. Nearly all had claw marks on the face, chest and stomach. Kondo knew the big cat had its eyes glued on him. If it was going to run away, it would have done so when it saw him.

"Lord," prayed Kondo under his breath, "protect me from this leopard."

The Africans have a great respect for leopards since it is difficult to tell what they will do. One time a leopard may turn and run away; another time it might wait in a tree or hide in a bush or in the grass, waiting for its prey. The older men of the village say that a leopard that attacks a person is one that needs to be killed as soon as possible. It is the belief that one attack will lead to another until its only victims are people.

The man and beast faced each other in the darkness. A mosquito had landed on Kondo's cheek, but any move by the African could send the vicious wild cat hurtling at him. Suddenly a grass mat over the doorway of a nearby hut moved and a man stepped out of the house. Distracted by the noise behind him, the leopard turned its head to look. Without wasting a second, the pastor yelled as loud as he could and ran, waving his arms, toward the animal. The workman looked and saw what was happening. He, too, took off in the direction of the leopard.

"Get out of here!" yelled Kondo. "Out of my way, you beast!"

The huge leopard took a giant leap and in seconds disappeared into the grass.

"Kondo! Are you all right?" It was Paul Davis, running up the path toward the workmen's village.

"I'm all right, Mr. Davis," responded the sweating pastor. "I really thought it had me. If it hadn't been for Moussa coming out of his house, I don't know what I would have done." Kondo quickly related what had happened.

"There's one thing for sure," Paul said, shaking his head, "this mission field is sure filled with excitement. One could write a book on what has happened around here."

"What things would you write about?" asked Kondo as he reached out to shake Moussa's hand.

"Well," Paul stood thinking, "it seems it really started when Dr. Simms and I were threatened by Chief Paul."

"That's over two years ago now," Kondo said, counting on his fingers. "But it doesn't seem very long, does it, Mr. Davis?"

"At times it does, Kondo, but other times it seems like only yesterday that we were attacked and your houses were burned."

"And Chief Paul was saved," added Kondo.

"What a change has taken place in this area," continued Paul.

"The story of Bio, Chief Ndeke's conversion and. . . ."

"Don't forget those mambas, Mr. Davis," interrupted the pastor, laughing.

"How can I ever forget that experience?" Paul agreed. "Well, as I said, someone should write a book about the things that have happened since that first encounter with Chief Paul."

"He was Ngonjo then," added Kondo.

"Right, 'Ngonjo,' " repeated the missionary, "but now, 'Chief Paul.' Ngonjo and Saul disappeared when Christ came in."

"Amen," whispered the pastor. "Amen."

31

Chief Paul's Gift

The days passed quickly in the busy preparations for the weddings. By the morning of September 24, several hundred people had arrived, settling in the villages surrounding Yanga Two. All kinds of foods were being brought in by the Africans. Some were giving their food as gifts while others were being paid. Once again, Chief Paul insisted that the cost of the feast be his, and that he personally be responsible for the food.

"Tene's my son and you missionaries are like my own children. What father wouldn't do this for his children?" he asked them when Paul tried to pay for a basket of manioc.

Chief Ndeke arrived with nearly half of his villagers. They had traveled for three days to get there. "We wouldn't miss this for anything," he said. "We have never seen foreigners get married before."

To ease the burden of walking for some of the villagers, Dale and Bill made a number of trips between Yanga One and Yanga Two. The dust-covered travelers welcomed the hastily constructed showers that Ken had put up at the back of the mission station.

That evening, Chief Paul was sitting on the front veranda of the mission house, chatting with Tene and Ruth and Paul and Ann. He asked if he could speak with the two couples alone. Even though the place was alive with people, no one ventured near the five friends as they talked. Paul mentioned the fact that the people were staying a good distance from them.

"That's because I asked for this time alone with you," explained Chief Paul. "All I had to do was tell a few, and in a short time the whole crowd out there knew that I would be meeting with the four of you. We have a good communications system."

The African smiled as he looked out among the visitors. "They respect a person's request for privacy," Chief Paul added. "But if you don't ask for it, then be prepared for anything but privacy. Your house is their house and they will come and go like family."

"Now, one of the things that I want to tell you is that you all have been very busy lately and I want to do something special for you. You would make me happy if you would accept the gift about which I will speak."

"You know I can't refuse you," said Tene, looking at his adopted father.

"I realize that, Tene. I'm speaking more to Mr. Davis than to you."

Paul glanced at Ann and then at the chief. "Knowing you as we do, Chief Paul, we will accept your gift."

The village leader clapped his hands. "Fine! The surprise is this. My people have been working secretly, making a road out to the river. That's about three hour's walk from my village. My men have built two beautiful mud block houses on each end of the long beach that is out there. I have arranged to post guards around the forests nearby for your protection as well as to be of help to you if you need them. Food will be brought to you every day. It will be your own village for two weeks. What do you think of our surprise?"

"A honeymoon," whispered Ann, placing her hand on Paul's arm. "What a wonderful place for a honeymoon. Why, we can do lots of things with Tene and Ruth."

"It will be fun," responded Tene. "You can tell us about your country and we can tell you more about ours and teach you more about our culture. I'll even teach you how to catch fish, Miss Ann."

Ann stood up and walked over to Chief Paul. She bent her head close to his, cupped her hands over her mouth and gently blew into his ear.

"You are one of us for sure," exclaimed the chief with a big grin. "Only a Banda can do that the way you did, Miss Ann."

Everyone retired very late that night. Morning came quickly

and with it the excitement of the wedding. Long before the sun poked its face over the distant hills, the people were sitting around their small fires, drinking their early coffee. During the night several hundred more visitors arrived, some having traveled for many miles. To feed such a large crowd, Chief Paul had had several women making manioc donuts for two days. Now the women were assigned the job of passing them out among the hungry people.

"How many have you made?" Chief Paul asked one of the cooks.

"Over six thousand," answered the weary but proud worker. "I've never seen so much food in all my life."

Another crew of women had been busy all night preparing food for the feast which was to follow the wedding. Making sure there were enough donuts and coffee for all, the chief then made his way over to the larger group of cooks. The workmen of Yanga Two had constructed long low rows of racks upon which were laid hundreds of pieces of chicken, beef and goat meat. The smoldering fire beneath not only cooked the meat slowly, but also kept it warm. A fifty-five gallon barrel was used for making the coffee. The aroma of food was everywhere and the atmosphere was festive.

"How are things out there?" Bill Dykes called to the African chief when he came into the house at mid-morning.

"Everything is fine, Mr. Dykes. I hope the people are hungry or there's going to be a lot of food around here for awhile."

By noon the yard between the dispensary and the mission house was filled. Because of the large crowd, it had been decided that the ceremony would be held out in the open on a platform so all could see. It was planned that Ann and Ruth would walk between two rows of children from the house to the platform. Chief Paul had brightly colored yellow and green dresses made for the girls, and shirts and pants to match for the boys.

In their meeting with the missionaries the day before, Chief Paul, Kondo and Tene had asked the missionaries to put as much American style as possible into the wedding ceremony.

"Our people just get the papers at the administrator's office and that's it," Chief Paul had said. "As long as a man pays the parents the asking price for the girl, the government issues him a marriage paper. With that in hand, he's married." The village leader had snapped his fingers to emphasize his point as to the time it takes.

"Of course, since you missionaries came you have been teaching us Christians to have a ceremony in church after the man gets the paper from the government office. We like that because marriage really is a union sanctioned by God."

At 12:45 the children took their places in line. "Shall I begin to play the organ now?" Dorothy Banks asked Marge. The folding pump organ had been carried from the mission house and placed on the platform. In order for all to hear it, Ken had placed one of the two microphones beside it. The organ music quieted the crowd as they awaited the event for which they had gathered.

At five minutes before one o'clock, Ken and Pastor Kondo, followed by Paul and Tene, approached the platform. Nearly two thousand people watched in silence. Dorothy played a hymn which the Africans knew and then began the "Wedding March." Slowly Ruth and Ann, dressed in beautiful gowns, began walking between the rows of children. Marge accompanied Ann while one of Ruth's cousins walked with her. Never before had the Africans seen anyone dressed like that for a wedding.

Reaching the platform, the four women were helped up the wooden steps. They made their way to a marked place on the floor which put them in front of Pastor Kondo and Ken. Paul stepped beside Ann and Tene beside Ruth. Dorothy stopped playing and the crowd remained silent.

Pastor Kondo spoke first. "Dear friends, we are here today to witness the joining of these two couples in holy marriage. Some of you have come a long way to witness this ceremony. Now, here we are and I'm convinced it is God's time for this marriage to take place."

There was a loud clicking of tongues as the pastor spoke. "With me is Dr. Simms. We look upon him most of the time as a doctor for our sicknesses. Dr. Simms is also a preacher. His church in America set him apart for that ministry. Together, we will conduct the ceremony."

Pastor Kondo read the Scripture and Ken talked about the Christian's responsibility in marriage. The pastor then led Tene and Ruth in their marriage vows, followed by Ken with Paul and Ann's vows. When both couples had completed their vows, Kondo and Ken pronounced each of the couples husband and wife.

"That was beautiful," Ann whispered to Paul as they turned to face the crowd.

"It really was, honey. This is new for most of them out there."

Before the two couples left the platform, Chief Paul made his way up the steps. He stood behind one of the microphones. "My people, listen to me."

The crowd became silent again. Every eye was fastened on the respected leader. "I've asked Mr. Dykes to say some words to you about something which is far better than the food you are going to eat. Listen to every word he has to say."

Bill stepped to the microphone. "Greetings, friends."

More tongue clicking came from the crowd.

"You are hungry, I know. The food that you are about to eat will satisfy your stomachs for a while. Tomorrow you will eat again. The food which I have here for you will satisfy your hearts for all time. Once you take it and believe it, you will have everlasting life."

Bill spoke for fifteen minutes, giving a clear message of Jesus being the Bread of Life. Ann's heart was thrilled as she watched the faces of the people. Now and then she could here Tene click his tongue or say "amen." When Bill finished, he asked all those who wanted to accept Christ to come forward and meet him in the yard behind the house. As those making decisions began to respond to the invitation, many of the Christian men and women of Yanga One and Yanga Two took this as their cue to come with them. The new believers needed someone to talk and pray with them, and the reaction of the Christians who came indicated the good teaching they had received.

Chief Paul then asked the people remaining to close their eyes while he prayed. And pray he did. The beloved chief prayed for those making decisions at that moment. He asked God's blessings on the two newly married couples. He thanked God for the missionaries and asked God to bless their time together. When the chief said "amen," a low hum could be heard throughout the crowd.

Chief Paul looked toward the women preparing the food. Cupping his hands to his mouth, he called, "Bring on the food! Let's begin our feast!"

Before long the sound of smacking lips and finger licking could be heard over most the mission station.

"They really enjoy their food," quipped Ken.

"I love to see them eat," added Marge.

"And hear them, too," said Bill, laughing.

Just then Paul and Ann appeared from the crowd. "Anyone for seconds?" called Paul. "Ann and I were over with the cooks and they've prepared enough food to feed an army."

Bill nudged Paul and pointed with his chin to a happy group of Christians sitting nearby.

"Just look at them, Paul. Every one of them represents a miracle of God."

"They sure do," responded Paul. "Chief Paul, Kondo, Chief Ndeke and John all have a story to tell—a fascinating story of God's grace."

32

The Last Sheep

Tene pointed to the two lumps rising out of the water about fifty feet away. The full African moon cast a silvery path across the still surface of the river, making it easier to see the strange visitor.

Ann huddled close to Paul. "What is it?" she whispered.

"It's either a large crocodile or a hippopotamus," answered Paul.

"It's a hippopotamus," responded Tene in a low voice. "If it were a crocodile, you would see its nose sticking out of the water along with its eyes."

"What are we going to do?" questioned Paul, keeping his eyes glued on the strange-looking objects which gave the appearance of two large warts on the surface of the still river.

"Stay right here," said Tene. "I think it sees us. If it comes much closer, we'll run farther up the beach. If necessary, we'll light some dried grass or shine a flashlight at it."

Just then there was a loud splash as the huge animal lifted its head out of the water. Ann and Ruth ran quickly toward one of the mud huts. The hippopotamus moved toward the shore where Paul and Tene still stood.

"We had better leave, Mr. Davis," spoke Tene, taking Paul by the arm. "That beast is serious."

Within seconds the men reached their wives and ran toward one of the huts. "Forget the flashlight!" shouted Tene. "Get in the truck. Hurry!"

Fortunately, the two couples had run toward the Davises' hut behind which was parked Paul's pickup. Paul and the two women got into the cab while Tene crawled up into the back of the pickup. Paul put the key in the ignition and started the engine. He turned the headlights on just in time to see the large African animal come into view not far from Tene's hut.

"He's blinded from the lights," called Tene. "Blow the horn, Mr. Davis."

Following the advice from his African friend, the missionary pressed on the horn button. The loud blare sent the beast lumbering toward Tene and Ruth's hut.

"He's going to hit. . . ." Tene's words were lost as the hippopotamus crashed blindly into the mud wall. The grass roof fell on top of the frightened animal, sending him scurrying toward the river. With a series of splashes, the beast disappeared into the water.

Paul left the engine running and the lights on and got out of the truck. He looked up at Tene, who was gazing off toward the river. "Now what was I saying?" asked Tene, with a strange grin. The four friends looked at each other and simultaneously broke into laughter.

"They'll never believe this story back in America," said Ann, still holding her hand to her mouth.

"They won't believe this story back in the village," added Tene. "Who would ever believe that we were chased by a hippopotamus and that he ran through our hut?"

Tene's words and the sound of his voice started the group laughing again. "Seriously," said Paul, "thank the Lord none of us was injured. I never want an experience like that again. What do we do now?"

"First of all," responded Tene, "let's see what damage the hippopotamus did to our things in the hut."

Paul got back in the truck and drove it to the destroyed hut. He carefully parked so the headlights would shine into the shamble.

"I'm glad we didn't bring many things with us, Tene," spoke Ruth, picking up a flattened, homemade plywood suitcase. "At least our clothes can't be crushed."

The couples salvaged what they could from the hut and carried the things over to Paul's and Ann's hut. "I suggest that the women sleep in the hut. You and I will sleep out here on the sand in front of the doorway, Mr. Davis," said Tene, motioning to a place in front of the hut. "That hippopotamus won't be back."

"But what about those hyenas and lions that we have been hearing this past week?" questioned Paul in a concerned voice. "Some of them have even come up to the sides of our huts."

"They're only a little curious, that's all," answered Tene, with his usual grin. "They are as afraid of you as you are of them."

The morning sun was a relief to Paul. He was sure he had not slept even fifteen minutes the entire night. He could not say the same for Tene, however. The young African slept soundly the whole night. Paul kidded him about it when his friend awoke.

"Now I know why you weren't afraid of any wild animals coming near us," laughed the missionary. "Why, you snored so loud, I'm sure you scared them off."

The two couples had breakfast of coffee, buns and fruit and then went back to see what more they could salvage from the hut. They decided that they would do some fishing and after lunch return to Yanga One. They would be two days earlier than they had planned, but they were eager to get back to the work.

"I hear a truck motor," said one of the men sitting by Chief Paul in front of the leader's house.

"If it's Tene and Paul, then I would say that something has happened to bring them home early or they got homesick to see us." The African chief laughed at his own remarks as he stood to his feet. By the time he reached the edge of the forest where the newly cut road came from the river, the blue pickup appeared from around the last bend in the road.

"There they are now," exclaimed Chief Paul. "I must admit, it's always nice to have my children return."

The next half hour brought hilarious laughter throughout Yanga One as Tene demonstrated over and over how he ran with the others to the truck for safety.

"I couldn't believe my eyes," he shouted above the laughter. "That big beast ran right through that hut, and for all we know it could be wearing my green pair of pants over it ears. We never did find them."

"You should have seen it jump when Paul blew the horn," said Ann, joining in the reporting.

Paul held up his hand for everyone's attention. "I think the thing that really brought me home early was Tene's snoring. He was worse than all the hyenas and lions put together."

Again the village erupted with laughter.

"What's going on here?" came a familiar voice. The excitement of the hippopotamus story and the noise of the villagers had muffled the sound of the Simms's truck. Ken and Marge slipped out of the truck and made their way to the large circle where the two couples shared the spotlight.

"Hello, Dr. Simms. Hello, Mrs. Simms," said Chief Paul, who finally noticed the newcomers. "We have just heard a tale which beats all tales. Our friends were chased by a hippopotamus and they scared it so badly it ran right through Tene's and Ruth's hut."

"And Tene thinks that the beast ran off with his green pants," added Paul, slapping his African friend on the shoulder. A burst of laughter followed and continued until Chief Paul signaled them to stop.

"Well, here we are again, my dear friends," spoke the village leader. "I think we should have a testimony time and just share again what God has done for us."

Within minutes the villagers gathered in a large circle. Several told of God's blessings upon their lives. The meeting had gone on for about an hour when one of the older men stood to his feet. In his crackling voice he began to speak. "My people, I am the oldest person in this village. I was already hunting, Chief Paul, when your mother, Bio, was born. As you know, I haven't said much of anything to any of you about the changes around here. I figured that sooner or later you would get tired of all this nonsense and get back to what your fathers taught you." The villagers sat in silence as the old man spoke.

"I've sat and watched all that has happened. I knew the secret of Martin Blanc. Bio forgot and let it slip in my presence one time. I never let on that I heard her. When she said she had Jesus in her heart, I thought our gods would destroy us all, but nothing happened."

Several laughed and clicked their tongues to indicate their agreement with the old man's words. "When that young white man there lost his wife to death but yet came back to live and work among us, I really began to hunt my heart about the whole thing. And that young white girl there. She didn't have to come here and live among us. She could have many more things in her own country. But now I know the answer to it all. We had a good laugh today about the hippopotamus chasing the four of them, but laughter is only for a day. Tomorrow it is gone and maybe sorrow and death has replaced it."

"I see a good sermon developing," Ken whispered to Marge. "You watch and listen. We are going to see another miracle at Yanga."

"I'm an old man. Soon I will die. But I'm not ready to die!" The startled villagers lifted their heads as the white-haired man cried out in his feeble voice. "Your God is the true God! Jesus is real! I've seen the truth in many of your lives and Ngonjo, uh . . . uh, Paul, over there is the greatest proof of all. No, he's not that mean old Ngonjo any more. He's changed and only the true God can do that."

The old man walked over to Tene and put his hand on the young pastor's shoulder. "Now, Tene, my heart is ready to go to His great village when I die."

Every head bowed in silent prayer as Tene prayed with the old man. By the time he had finished praying, the sun had slipped behind the dry season haze, casting a beautiful rose hue upon the village of Yanga. By head count, Chief Paul knew that his prayer had been answered. The old man was the last person who needed to be saved at Yanga One!